Family
RESTORATION

MALACHI DADS

D0062394

Family
RESTORATION

MALACHI DADS

1 East Bode Road
Streamwood, IL 60107-6658 U.S.A.
awana.org
(630) 213-2000

1   2   3   4   5   6   21   20   19   18   17   16

CONTENTS

SUMMARY

JEREMIAH'S WORLD — INTRODUCTION

Jeremiah worked tirelessly in the hope that he could lead his people out of their messed-up thinking and back to a healthy standing with God and with each other. He encouraged the people to use their time of captivity to prepare themselves for the day when they would be restored to their land and their people.

APPLICATION

As you've worked through the Malachi Dads™ program, you've seen how important it is to be involved in the lives of your children during your incarceration. Now it's time to take some practical steps to prepare yourself to build a healthy family structure once you are released.

In this study, we'll explore the ancient world of Jeremiah's time in order to find some words and warnings to help lead you along the journey toward healthy relationships.

LESSON 1 **MEMORY VERSE**

I press on toward the goal for the prize of the upward call of God in Christ Jesus.

(Philippians 3:14)

INTRODUCTION

DAY 1 | REVIEW

Malachi Dads Pledge

As a Malachi Dad, I solemnly pledge to glorify God and build His kingdom by prioritizing the raising of godly children, first in my family, then in the influencing of other men to do the same in theirs. I firmly believe that my transformed life in Christ — my life of integrity, pursuit of this vision, and the pursuit of godly character — will allow me to impact my children, family, and others towards this end.

I will practice a life of daily discipline and dependence on God through prayer and the study of God's Word for the wisdom in how to "nurture my children in the admonition of the Lord." I will pursue this endeavor for a lifetime whether my children are in my home or not.

Finally, I believe that my end goal is not only for my children to walk in the Lord but that this God-given vision would impact multiple generations to come.

So help me God.

As we continue the journey of Malachi Dads, take a moment to look at both the present and the future.

What opportunities do you have now to love and guide your children?

What steps can you take now to prepare yourself to be reunited with your children?

Please don't be deceived. You won't find a perfect life outside your prison bars and gates. Freedom won't make you free from all problems and pain. Family life is hard. Parenting is hard. Surviving in this world is hard — which means you have work to do.

God wants to restore your family. Just as you've taken hold of your responsibilities as a father, you must now take hold of your responsibility to do whatever is in your power to create a healthier life for your family. Are you ready to roll up your sleeves?

Throughout this study, we will use the prophet Jeremiah as a model for godly living in captivity. Jeremiah's world was a mess. He had a number of problems to deal with — including war, false prophets, and the call to preach God's message to people who didn't want to hear it.

Worst of all, he lost his freedom. Jeremiah was forced to deal with these troubles while living as a captive in a foreign land.

FALSE WORSHIP

Before beginning Jeremiah's story, we'll spend this first week exploring several false ideas that were common among God's people in Jeremiah's day. Why? Because these false ideas are also common among God's people today. These false thoughts can derail our efforts to follow God — as well as cause spiritual damage within our families.

We'll get started with false ideas about worship. Take a look at Jeremiah 7:21-28.

How would you summarize God's message in these verses?

Thus says the LORD of hosts, the God of Israel: "Add your burnt offerings to your sacrifices, and eat the flesh. For in the day that I brought them out of the land of Egypt, I did not speak to your fathers or command them concerning burnt offerings and sacrifices. But this command I gave them: 'Obey My voice, and I will be your God, and you shall be My people. And walk in all the way that I command you, that it may be well with you.' But they did not obey or incline their ear, but walked in their own counsels and the stubbornness of their evil hearts, and went backward and not forward. From the day that your fathers came out of the land of Egypt to this day, I have persistently sent all My servants the prophets to them, day after day. Yet they did not listen to Me or incline their ear, but stiffened their neck. They did worse than their fathers. So you shall speak all these words to them, but they will not listen to you. You shall call to them, but they will not answer you. And you shall say to them, 'This is the nation that did not obey the voice of the LORD their God, and did not accept discipline; truth has perished; it is cut off from their lips.' "

How do these verses reveal God's patience?

The first part of this passage tells us the people of Jeremiah's day were still making an effort to obey God's law. They went to worship services, offered sacrifices, and did what the priests told them to do. But their hearts weren't in it. They thought that going through the motions of religious practices meant God would be pleased with them — but He wasn't.

Instead, God reminded His people about all the times they had ignored Him and rejected Him. God said they were stiff-necked. This was a farming term. It referred to cattle that refused to let their master place a yoke over their necks and connect them to the plow. The animal stiffened its neck in stubbornness and fought against its master's will, which made it useless.

If we're not careful, the same can happen to us. Going to church, reading our Bibles, and doing other religious things won't do us any good if we stubbornly fight against God's will.

ASSIGNMENT

Use the following questions to evaluate your own experiences with God:

What religious habits or practices in your life are in danger of becoming stale?

What's an area in which you are resisting or avoiding God's will?

DAY 2 | FALSE SECURITY

As we saw yesterday, the people of Judah experienced all kinds of chaos during the early parts of Jeremiah's ministry. Most importantly, they were threatened with war by the Babylonians — a ruthless and powerful people.

In the middle of the chaos, the religious leaders of Judah told everyone to relax. They claimed everything would be fine. They believed that nothing bad could happen to them or their city because the temple of God was standing within their gates. Surely God would never let anything bad happen to His own house!

Here's what God had to say, speaking through the prophet Jeremiah: "... *Hear the word of the LORD, all you men of Judah who enter these gates to worship the LORD. Thus says the LORD of hosts, the God of Israel: Amend your ways and your deeds, and I will let you dwell in this place. Do not trust in these deceptive words: 'This is the temple of the LORD, the temple of the LORD, the temple of the LORD.' For if you truly amend your ways and your deeds, if you truly execute justice one with another, if you do not oppress the sojourner, the fatherless, or the widow, or shed innocent blood in this place, and if you do not go after other gods to your own harm, then I will let you dwell in this place, in the land that I gave of old to your fathers forever. Behold, you trust in deceptive words to no avail*" (Jeremiah 7:2-8).

What warnings did God give His people?

What did God expect from His people?

Later in Chapter 7, God reminded the people of Judah about an earlier time when God allowed His house of worship to be destroyed (see verses 12-15). When the Israelites first conquered the Promised Land, they set up the tabernacle — the tent of worship — at a place called Shiloh. This is where God's presence dwelt among His people.

When the people continually disobeyed God, however, He allowed the Philistines to conquer Shiloh before the time of King Saul. The Philistines even captured the Ark of the Covenant, which was a powerful symbol of God's presence and holiness.

Jeremiah's point was clear: if God had allowed His dwelling place to be destroyed at Shiloh because His people were disobedient, the same thing could happen in Jerusalem. The people of Judah had a false sense of security. They were rebelling against God and doing evil, yet they thought God would protect them because of the temple. They were wrong.

What about you? What are you relying on as a source of security that's separate from God? Some people bank on money as a source of safety. Others rely on drugs or alcohol to give them false protection from pain and suffering. Still others seek to look as tough as possible and rely on their own strength to take care of themselves. Like the Israelites, many Christians keep up with religious rituals and practices in order to convince themselves that God is on their side.

All of these lead down the same road: a false security that results in destruction.

When have you been burned by trusting in something or someone that wasn't reliable?

How have you benefitted from trusting in God?

ASSIGNMENT

Whenever you pray this week, spend a few moments asking God to show you any places in your life where you're looking for safety and security outside of Him. Consider writing down what God reveals to you as a way of keeping yourself accountable.

DAY 3 | FALSE HOPE

Hope is often a good and helpful quality. Hope can give us strength even in the middle of tough times. But hope can also be dangerous — especially when we hope for things that go against God's will. That's what the people of Jerusalem discovered in Jeremiah's day.

When we look at Jeremiah 24, we can see right away that the situation had gotten worse for God's people: *After Nebuchadnezzar king of Babylon had taken into exile from Jerusalem Jeconiah the son of Jehoiakim, king of Judah, together with the officials of Judah, the craftsmen, and the metal workers, and had brought them to Babylon, the LORD showed me this vision: behold, two baskets of figs placed before the temple of the LORD. One basket had very good figs, like first-ripe figs, but the other basket had very bad figs, so bad that they could not be eaten. And the LORD said to me, "What do you see, Jeremiah?" I said, "Figs, the good figs very good, and the bad figs very bad, so bad that they cannot be eaten"* (Jeremiah 24:1-3).

Ignore the figs for a moment and concentrate on that first verse. The king, the officials, and all the skilled workers of Judah had been taken captive and carried off to Babylon. This was a major blow to God's people. They had been defeated and humiliated by their enemies.

Yet, amazingly, the false prophets in Jerusalem were still claiming that everything would be OK. They told the remaining people that God would arrange a quick and speedy release of the captives in

Babylon. They had hope in God's power to rescue them, but their disobedience had blinded them to the fact that God was no longer on their side.

Back to the figs. God gave Jeremiah a metaphor (an object lesson) to help counter the words of the false prophets. Jeremiah was shown two baskets of figs — one with very good figs and one with very bad figs. Here's what happened next: *Then the word of the LORD came to me: "Thus says the LORD, the God of Israel: Like these good figs, so I will regard as good the exiles from Judah, whom I have sent away from this place to the land of the Chaldeans. I will set My eyes on them for good, and I will bring them back to this land. I will build them up, and not tear them down; I will plant them, and not pluck them up. I will give them a heart to know that I am the LORD, and they shall be My people and I will be their God, for they shall return to Me with their whole heart. But thus says the LORD: Like the bad figs that are so bad they cannot be eaten, so will I treat Zedekiah the king of Judah, his officials, the remnant of Jerusalem who remain in this land, and those who dwell in the land of Egypt. I will make them a horror to all the kingdoms of the earth, to be a reproach, a byword, a taunt, and a curse in all the places where I shall drive them. And I will send sword, famine, and pestilence upon them, until they shall be utterly destroyed from the land that I gave to them and their fathers"* (Jeremiah 24:4-10).

What was going to happen to the good figs?

What was going to happen to the bad figs?

How would you describe the meaning of this metaphor?

Through Jeremiah, God showed the people of Judah that He is the only source of true hope. It seemed like the captives in Babylon were in worse shape than the people left in Jerusalem. But God knew the captives would learn from their experience and turn back to Him — while the people of Jerusalem would continue to rely on false hope and ultimately wither away.

The same is true for you. Even in captivity, you are not abandoned. If you place your hope in God, you will win out in the end.

ASSIGNMENT

What lessons have you learned during your time in prison? What has God taught you about yourself and about the world? Record your thoughts below.

1.

2.

3.

DAY 4 | FALSE REALITY

There are many parallels between Jeremiah's world and the world of an incarcerated person. For example, the people taken captive to Babylon experienced the consequences of poor choices — specifically, of choosing to live in rebellion against God. It wasn't God's intention for His people to worship idols and adopt evil practices, but He didn't stop them from doing so. He allowed them to experience captivity because of their choices.

What are some choices or practices in your life that led you to prison?

Thankfully, God still cared for His people after they were taken into captivity. He still loved them, and He had a plan to rescue them. He used their time in Babylon to prepare them for their future freedom.

What are some ways people can be taken captive or held prisoner in the outside world?

How has God been preparing you to serve Him both in prison and outside?

Jeremiah has some serious lessons to teach God's people today. He used strong language to make his points, so brace yourself — the prophet will seem in your face at times. But his main message to the people of Judah is something you need to hear as well: Don't waste your captivity. When you turn to the Lord, you can be restored from your captivity to a place of greater peace and productivity.

As you work through this study, you will use Jeremiah's messages to identify healthy principles for you and your family.

ASSIGNMENT

Take some time to reread Jeremiah 24:1-10. Write down your thoughts on how these verses apply to your current situation.

DAY 5 | AVOIDING A FALSE START

Digging through the Old Testament can feel difficult for modern readers — especially engaging the Old Testament prophets. If you've felt lost or confused during the past week, don't let it bother you. The more you learn about Jeremiah and his world in the days to come, the more you'll hear what God has to say through the powerful words of His prophet.

In the meantime, spend a few minutes reviewing the material you've covered this week. Feel free to look through the earlier pages of this study as you answer the following questions.

1. **In what city did Jeremiah preach and prophesy?**

2. **What was the name of the nation whose armies attacked God's people and took them into captivity?**

3. **How were God's people going through the motions in their worship?**

4. Why did the people of Jerusalem think the temple would keep them safe from attack?

5. In Jeremiah 24, what did the good figs represent? What about the bad figs?

ASSIGNMENT

Take a moment to think about the next 11 weeks of this study. What do you hope to learn or experience in that time?

Review this week's memory verse — Philippians 3:14 — on page 8. Work on studying the Scripture until you can write it down from memory.

SUMMARY

JEREMIAH'S WORLD — CAPTIVITY

The prophet Jeremiah wrote letters to those who had already been taken into Babylonian captivity. His message to them was to stop fighting against God and stop putting their hopes in a quick rescue. The captivity was something God had initiated, which meant His people had something to gain from it.

APPLICATION

The degree of your restoration is going to be dependent on what you learn during your captive years. Don't waste this time! Now is the chance to learn and practice healthy relationship skills that will strengthen your relationships with your children and other family members.

LESSON 2 **MEMORY VERSE**

For I know the plans I have for you, declares the LORD, plans for welfare and not for evil, to give you a future and a hope.

(Jeremiah 29:11)

Lesson 2

THE YEARS OF CAPTIVITY

DAY 1 | REVIEW

Malachi Dads Pledge

As a Malachi Dad, I solemnly pledge to glorify God and build His kingdom by prioritizing the raising of godly children, first in my family, then in the influencing of other men to do the same in theirs. I firmly believe that my transformed life in Christ — my life of integrity, pursuit of this vision, and the pursuit of godly character — will allow me to impact my children, family, and others towards this end.

I will practice a life of daily discipline and dependence on God through prayer and the study of God's Word for the wisdom in how to "nurture my children in the admonition of the Lord." I will pursue this endeavor for a lifetime whether my children are in my home or not.

Finally, I believe that my end goal is not only for my children to walk in the Lord but that this God-given vision would impact multiple generations to come.

So help me God.

DAY 1 | GOD'S PLANS

As a correctional minister, I use some form of Jeremiah 29:11 almost daily. In the prison setting, I deal with broken individuals who feel discarded by society. Many of them are buckling under the weight of their own guilt and can't see past their regrets and consequences.

Could there be any sweeter words for such persons than to hear that God still has a purpose for their lives? They need to know that He is not done with them and has not discarded them no matter what. It's not over, and all is not lost. There is always hope of redemption!

What about you?

How does the promise of Jeremiah 29:11 apply to your life?

Whom can you share that promise with as an act of encouragement?

Jeremiah 29:11 offers good news, but we must be careful not to take it out of context and skip over what God's Word is really speaking. We need to be confident that, when we speak the promise of Jeremiah 29:11, we do so in the spirit it was intended.

ASSIGNMENT

To make sure you have a proper understanding of Jeremiah 29:11, read the entire chapter of Jeremiah 29. Tomorrow we will look at the context of that chapter, including the original audience to which it was given.

DAY 2 | JEREMIAH'S WORLD

By the time of the prophet Jeremiah's day, God's people long had been in stubborn rebellion. They mistakenly believed that God would not call them out or punish them because they were His chosen people.

While the nation of Babylon breathed down their necks, the people of Judah falsely put their hope in the presence of the temple, believing that God would never let anything happen to His sacred house (see Jeremiah 7:1-15). And while the prophet Jeremiah proclaimed the soon-coming destruction of the temple and Jerusalem around it, false prophets gave the misleading hope of God's protection without any conditions.

Get started by reading the first chapter of Jeremiah. Write down any phrases of reassurance God gave to Jeremiah.

God encouraged Jeremiah a great deal because his ministry would be so difficult. In fact, here's the message Jeremiah was supposed to deliver to his own people: *Then the LORD said to me, "Out of the north disaster shall be let loose upon all the inhabitants of the land. For behold, I am calling all the tribes of the kingdoms of the north, declares the LORD, and they shall come, and every one shall set his throne at the entrance of the gates of Jerusalem, against all its walls all around and against all the cities of Judah. And I will declare my judgments against them, for all their evil in forsaking me. They have made offerings to other gods and worshiped the works of their own hands" (Jeremiah 1:14-16).*

In your own words, summarize what Jeremiah was supposed to preach.

It goes without saying that Jeremiah was not a popular prophet. Everyone, even his own family, hated him for his messages of judgment and defeat of their nation at the hands of the Babylonians. They much preferred the false prophets' message that God would rescue them and deliver them from their enemies.

Not surprisingly, Jeremiah didn't enjoy being the bearer of bad news. He actually despised his assignment from the Lord (see Jeremiah 20:7-18). But no matter how hard it got, Jeremiah remained faithful.

We have a faithful God who does not leave or forsake us. He is calling us to reflect His faithfulness to our families. Our job as parents is not easy. Are you willing to be faithful and obedient, trusting that God will fight for you and be with you and rescue you (Jeremiah 1:19)?

ASSIGNMENT

It was vital for Jeremiah to speak and live the truth even when it would cause him hardship. The same is true for you as a parent.

How is the call to serve as a godly parent similar to the call Jeremiah received?

What attitudes and disciplines will be necessary to speak and live the truth for the benefit of your children?

DAY 3 | THE IMPACT OF THE PROMISE

Though Jeremiah's ministry was to those living in Jerusalem, a portion of God's people had already been taken into exile to Babylon as captives (see Jeremiah 1:3). At some point, Jeremiah wrote a letter to those living as captives in Babylon.

Read Jeremiah 29:1-23 to see the contents of that letter. What stands out to you about Jeremiah's words?

Jeremiah told the captives to marry, buy houses, plant gardens, and basically settle into life in Babylon. Remember, the people of Babylon were considered enemies of God. False prophets among the Israelites were telling the people in exile that God would soon deliver them out of their enemy's hand. Jeremiah said the opposite. He even told them to pray for the prosperity of Babylon! How appalling that must have been to the captives!

It is in the context of this letter that the promise of 29:11 was given. In other words, Jeremiah was telling the exiles to settle in and make the most of life in captivity, but he also made clear that the captivity would not last forever. As a matter of fact, it would last for 70 years, at which time God would bring His people back to the land and restore them. Why? Because God had a plan to prosper them and give them a future.

Notice how the promise was connected with the people's obedience. Their captivity would lead the Israelites to turn from their sin and seek God. When they did, they would find Him. Their captivity was a consequence of their rebellion, but that didn't mean God had abandoned them. He was still with them.

The good news is that there's hope even in the midst of the darkest captivity. God can bring you back no matter how far you've wandered.

How has your time of incarceration impacted your relationship with God?

Just as with those of Jeremiah's day, sometimes it takes a drastic prison sentence to finally get a person to respond to God. At the moment, we want to cry out, "Why, God?" But deep down, we know why. We know that a long line of rebellion came before the time of incarceration.

Jeremiah explained that the exile of the Israelites was designed to turn them back to God. In the same way, a prison sentence forces a man to sit and think about his life. It gives him a chance to hear from God, submit to His plan, and enjoy His blessings even while in captivity.

ASSIGNMENT

Take a moment to sketch a timeline of the major events in your life leading up to your incarceration. Also write down times when you sensed God's voice urging you to turn to Him.

DAY 4 | YOUR POTENTIAL

If we use the promise of Jeremiah 29:11 as a blanket statement that applies to everyone, we misuse the Scriptures. This was a specific promise given to God's people during the Babylonian captivity.

Even so, the promise does communicate a universal and timeless truth — namely, that people who seek the Lord with sincerity and turn away from their sin can take assurance in the truth that God has a plan and a purpose for their lives. God can use even captivity as a way to draw us close to Himself.

The first part of Jeremiah 29:11 states, *For I* [the Lord] *know the plans I have for you.* Only God knows those plans. Therefore, the only way we can know those plans is to seek Him. If a man isn't interested in seeking the Lord, he forfeits the right to know the future and hope God has for him.

What steps have you taken in recent weeks to seek God and His plan for your life?

Look again at the context of the promise in Jeremiah 29:10-14. Write down the actions the people would take and the actions God would take.

Actions of the People   **Actions of God**

When we find people who are truly looking to be in fellowship with God, we can share the promise of Jeremiah 29:11 as an encouragement. The larger point of this passage is that, although we must bear the consequences of our actions, we don't have to lose hope — in fact, we shouldn't lose hope. Just as with the people of Jeremiah's day, God can use the valley of our bad decisions to make us stronger and bring us out of captivity closer to Him than we would have thought possible.

Make a comparison between your situation and that of the nation of Judah.

God's People in Judah	You
Sentence: 70 years	*Sentence:*
Place of exile: Babylon	*Place of exile:*
Disobedience: Worship of foreign gods	*Disobedience:*

The remainder of this study is written to help you settle into your current captivity, live at peace where you are, and use this time to turn back to the Lord. Your success will be determined by your commitment to those goals. Remember, don't waste your time in captivity.

Jeremiah's message to the exiles was that they would be better off than those not taken into exile. In other words, the free people of Jerusalem ended up dying because of their own sin. The exiles, the ones taken into captivity, actually had a chance to get things right and be restored back to God.

Are you willing to take advantage of your time in captivity? Will you let God use this time to transform you into something powerful — someone useful to Him and to your family? The choice is yours.

ASSIGNMENT

Write down specific ways you can make wise use of your time in captivity to seek the Lord and move forward toward restoration.

What can you do this week?

What can you do within the next month?

What can you do within the next year?

DAY 5 | REVIEW

To make sure we have a clear understanding of the message, today's lesson will help you review the information covered in Jeremiah 29. Take advantage of this opportunity to make sure you stay connected with the overall message of Jeremiah.

Where was Jeremiah when he wrote his letter to the exiles?

What did God want Jeremiah to say to the Israelites — both in Jerusalem and in captivity?

What did Jeremiah want the exiles to do in Babylon?

How did the false prophets attempt to lead God's people astray?

As we've seen throughout this week, the people of Jeremiah's day didn't want to hear what he had to say — what God had to say through him. They hated both the message and the messenger.

In the same way, perhaps you are less than excited about attempting to view your incarceration in a positive light. Please hear me when I say this: it's worth a try. By using your time in captivity to seek the Lord and His purpose for your life, you will make the most of the time ahead and be ready when God brings about your restoration.

ASSIGNMENT

Review your memory verse — Jeremiah 29:11. See if you can write it below from memory.

MALACHI DADS PLEDGE

As a Malachi Dad, I solemnly pledge to glorify God and build His kingdom by prioritizing the raising of godly children, first in my family, then in the influencing of other men to do the same in theirs. I firmly believe that my transformed life in Christ — my life of integrity, pursuit of this vision, and the pursuit of godly character — will allow me to impact my children, family, and others towards this end.

I will practice a life of daily discipline and dependence on God through prayer and the study of God's Word, for the wisdom in how to "nurture my children in the admonition of the Lord." I will pursue this endeavor for a lifetime whether my children are in my home or not.

Finally, I believe that my end goal is not only for my children to walk in the Lord, but that this God-given vision would impact multiple generations to come.

So help me God.

SUMMARY

JEREMIAH'S WORLD — SETTLING IN: HEALTY COMMUNICATION

Jeremiah told the people in captivity to settle down into life in Babylon. God wanted them to *seek the welfare of the city (Jeremiah 29:7).* During this time, they were instructed to seek the Lord, to go to Him and pray to Him, and then they would find Him.

APPLICATION

Your time of incarceration should be used to seek the Lord and learn His ways. This lesson will demonstrate how to use the prison setting to learn good communication skills that will be helpful during and after incarceration. Healthy communication is an important key to healthy families.

LESSON 3 **MEMORY VERSE**

Let no corrupting talk come out of your mouths, but only such as is good for building up, as fits the occasion, that it may give grace to those who hear.

(Ephesians 4:29)

SETTLING IN: HEALTHY COMMUNICATION

DAY 1 | COMMUNICATION OPPORTUNITIES

As we actively pursue our relationship with God, we want to work on our relationship with others. Luke 2:52 says: *And Jesus increased in wisdom and in stature and in favor with God and man.* We, too, want to develop mentally, physically, and progress in how we relate to God and others.

God has wired all people to be in relationships — even men. Our hearts naturally seek out connections with others, both through friendship and family. My work in a prison has taught me this truth more than any psychology textbook could have. Every day I see inmates join together in groups as a way of dealing with the realities of prison life. Sometimes these groups create negative consequences, such as codependence and abuse. But when washed in the truths of God's Word, community becomes an important tool for developing healthy relationships.

What are some of the challenges involved with building relationships in prison?

How have you benefited from relationships with others during your incarceration?

With all of this in mind, I propose that you use your time of incarceration as an opportunity to practice healthy relationships — with the ultimate goal of improving your ability to build and maintain relationships within your family. Later in this lesson, we'll explore the biblical definition of family and look at each member's role within the family unit. For now, however, we'll get started with something more basic: communication.

Whether you want to or not, you must interact with others in your institution every day: your roommate, the guards, people classified in the same work area, and so on. The communication tips we'll cover tomorrow will be beneficial not only to healthy families, but can also work to create healthy relationships in every area of life.

So begin preparing yourself for tomorrow as we begin to discover what the Bible has to say about healthy communication.

ASSIGNMENT

To start your preparation, talk with a few of the people you interact with. Ask them to give you feedback on your communication skills — good, bad, clear, unclear, and so on. Remember not to get angry if their answers aren't what you expect!

DAY 2 | COMMUNICATION QUESTIONS

As a prophet, Jeremiah was charged with speaking the words of God to the people of Judah. Therefore, communication was an essential skill. In the same way, you have a role in sharing truth with the people around you — including the members of your family.

Gain a better understanding of the biblical approach to communication by starting with this important passage of Scripture: *Let no corrupting talk come out of your mouths, but only such as is good for building up, as fits the occasion, that it may give grace to those who hear (Ephesians 4:29).*

This one verse offers a basic tool for improving our communication. We need to train ourselves to filter everything that pops into our mind through this verse before we let it out of our mouth. We can do this by asking ourselves three important questions before we speak.

Here's the first question: Is it necessary? Paul wrote, *Let no corrupting talk come out of your mouths.* Certainly, anything corrupt is something that doesn't need to be said — it's not necessary. Therefore, we need to make a special effort to eliminate those types of speech.

Read Ephesians 5:3-4. What comes to mind when you think about *crude joking*?

There are many people who will tell you that obscene conversation is just part of the prison culture — you can't avoid it. But what does God's Word say? If you truly wish to submit to God's authority, then you must put away immoral talk.

Here's the second question: Is it true? Sometimes we use empty words to flatter others in an attempt to manipulate the person or situation. Other times we flat out lie about others to make us feel better about ourselves. In order to communicate in a biblical way, we need to concentrate on speaking the truth.

In what situations are you tempted to speak falsehoods?

Here's the third question: Is it beneficial to building up others? As followers of God, we should take every opportunity we can find to use our words to build up others. This is helpful in a prison setting, where many people feel discouraged. But this practice is also critical within families.

Read Proverbs 16:24. What effect do gracious or pleasant words have on a person?

ASSIGNMENT

Ephesians 4:29 is your memory verse for this week. Use the following assessment to evaluate your speech. Where can you improve?

How confident do you feel in your ability to avoid corrupt, crude, or unnecessary words?

1   2   3   4   5   6   7   8   9   10
(Not confident)   (Confident)

How often do you struggle with saying things that aren't true?

1   2   3   4   5   6   7   8   9   10
(Not Often)   (Often)

How often do you intentionally use words to encourage those around you?

1   2   3   4   5   6   7   8   9   10
(Not Often)   (Often)

DAY 3 | COMMUNICATION

The Bible tells us our tongues, our speech, are more powerful than we may realize: *Death and life are in the power of the tongue, and those who love it will eat its fruits (Proverbs 18:21).*

How have you seen people's words produce death in the lives of others?

How have you seen people's words produce life?

Think about how the words of others have affected you. As a father, you want to choose your words toward your children carefully. Harshness and criticism are contagious in families. If this was how you were brought up, you will need to be deprogrammed in how you talk to others.

How would you describe the communication styles modeled in your family when you were a child?

The truth of the matter is that we talk more harshly to those we love. We feel that they love and accept us. Therefore, we don't have to be so careful not to hurt their feelings or offend them. Nothing could be further from the truth! Our words to our family members carry even greater power to build up or tear down.

So be on guard. Ask God to convict you when you speak harshly to those you love.

You've heard the old saying, "If you don't have anything nice to say, don't say anything at all." This is good advice, although it's not always possible to carry out. For example, the prophet Jeremiah was commanded to say some difficult things to the people of Judah. His message was harsh at times, yet his words came from a desire to see his people repent of their sin and return to God.

As a father, remember that you have the power of death and life in the words you speak to your children. Choose wisely.

ASSIGNMENT

After your next conversation with your family, take a moment to evaluate how things went. Did you speak positively? Did you say the things you wanted to say? Did you say anything you regret?

Record your thoughts from that conversation below.

Ask yourself the same questions about recent conversations with your friends and neighbors in prison. How would you evaluate your communication right now?

DAY 4 | COMMUNICATION RESPONSES

Part of godly communication is knowing how to respond to negative experiences — knowing what to say and knowing what not to say. Jeremiah dealt with people who pushed him toward a war of words, yet the prophet stayed true to his message.

We can do the same.

Read the following verses and summarize the main point of each.

James 1:19-20:

Psalm 141:3-4:

James 3:9-10:

Whether in prison or with your family, you will be tempted to use words in a negative way. This is especially true when others attack you with their words. You can work on growing as a communicator by making a plan to respond well in those situations — and by sticking to that plan.

ASSIGNMENT

Use the space below to write out at least four steps you will take when others push you to speak in a negative way.

1.

2.

3.

4.

DAY 5 | COMMUNICATION CHALLENGE

I estimate that about 95 percent of the problems in my prison would be resolved if we all could keep our mouths shut! I am referring to inmates, security, administration, and everyone in between.

There is a reason God gave us two ears and one mouth. We should listen twice as much as we speak! Sadly, we typically have it the other way around.

As a way to practice what you've learned about godly communication this week, take the following two challenges.

Review Challenge: Read Proverbs 10:19 once again. Reflect over the past 24 hours and write down any words spoken by others that have hurt you or affected you in a negative way.

Now write down any way your own words may have caused someone else harm or pain.

Silence Challenge: Choose a four-hour block of time (not in the middle of your sleeping hours) and practice remaining in complete silence. Instead of talking, listen closely to the conversations of others all around you. Record your observations below.

ASSIGNMENT

Review your memory verse for this week: Ephesians 4:29. See if you can write it below from memory.

Lesson 4

SUMMARY

JEREMIAH'S WORLD — SETTLING IN: AUTHORITY

Jeremiah told the people in captivity to settle down into life in Babylon and *seek the welfare of the city.* More, he specifically told them to submit to the authority of the wicked Babylonian leaders (see Jeremiah 27:8-11). In doing so, God promised to honor their submission and restore them to their land.

APPLICATION

An attitude of submission is a Christian characteristic that we all must embrace and is essential in order to be a strong family.

LESSON 4 **MEMORY VERSE**

Submitting to one another out of reverence for Christ.

(Ephesians 5:21)

Lesson 4

SETTLING IN: AUTHORITY

DAY 1 | COMMUNICATION OPPORTUNITIES

What does it mean to make Jesus the Lord of your life? It means you die to self. You give yourself away. He has the right to run your life.

As followers of Christ, we submit to His authority over us, knowing that His way for us is always best. To rebel against that authority is to run away from what we need most.

As fathers, we want our children to submit to our parental authority. Why? Because we believe we know better how to live life than our children. We have a greater understanding of how things are, and we want them to learn and grow from our wisdom.

So it is with God: *For My thoughts are not your thoughts, neither are your ways My ways, declares the LORD. For as the heavens are higher than the earth, so are My ways higher than your ways and My thoughts than your thoughts (Isaiah 55:8-9).*

What's your initial reaction to these verses? Why?

When have you seen evidence that God is more qualified to run your life than you are?

When it comes down to it, all sin is rebellion against God. That's because I is at the middle of our sin. We say, "I will do this my way, not God's, because I know better than God."

As we'll see tomorrow in the book of Jeremiah, such rebellion against God is always a bad idea.

ASSIGNMENT

It's not easy to give up control in our lives, but it's necessary for following Jesus. Use the space below to record areas of life where you find it most difficult to submit to God's authority.

DAY 2 | ISRAEL'S REBELLION

Start today by reading Jeremiah 2:1-13. How did Jeremiah describe the people's relationship with God in verses 1-3?

Though they had done nothing to earn God's favor, the people of Judah were God's chosen people and blessed as His covenant people. God fought their battles for them and destroyed their enemies.

In verses 4-8, God laid out His case against the Israelites, His people.

How would you summarize God's argument in verses 4-8?

The people of Judah had rejected God's blessings and instead responded with rebellion. Jeremiah stated that they ... went after worthlessness [false idols] and became worthless (v. 5b).

I've seen this progression so many times. Some people have every opportunity to know God and enjoy His fellowship, yet they rejected God's love and grace and ran after the worthless gods this world offers. In those situations, it doesn't take long before such people begin to reflect the worthlessness of what the world offers and leave far behind the glory of God.

After laying out His case, God brought charges against His people. Take a moment to read verses 9-13 again. Notice the two-fold action described in verse 13.

How would you describe the first sin mentioned in verse 13?

How would you describe the second sin?

Let's take a look at the comparison between a spring and a cistern. In the Judean area where Jeremiah lived, water was available in one of three forms. The first and best was living water. This type of water is fresh, such as a spring from the ground. Have you ever had water straight from a spring? It's the clearest and freshest water you have ever tasted!

The second option for water in Judea was from a well. One would dig deep into the ground to access the water table below the earth. The water could be lifted out and brought to the surface by a bucket on a rope.

The third option for water was from a cistern. A cistern was a deep channel or pit dug in the ground and then plastered so that the walls and bottom of the cistern would not leak. There was and still is very little rainfall in the Judean region. The purpose of these cisterns was to catch the runoff of water whenever it did rain. These deep cisterns would often be filled with years-old, stagnant rainwater that could be used for drinking and cooking. The cisterns were open for anything to fall into and rest at the bottom of the collected water. To make matters worse, sometimes the plaster walls of the cistern would crack and then the water you worked so hard to save would seep into the earth.

Now that you know the difference between springs of living water and cisterns, you can catch a sense of the terrible exchange the people of Judah made by rejecting the living God in favor of dead, worthless idols.

ASSIGNMENT

What are some idols people worship today in exchange for the living God? Write down at least three.

1.

2.

3.

DAY 3 | HUMAN AUTHORITY

The people of Judah in Jeremiah's day chose to actively rebel against God. In return, the prophet didn't pull any punches in describing their unfaithfulness: *For long ago I broke your yoke and burst your bonds; but you said, "I will not serve." Yes, on every high hill and under every green tree you bowed down like a whore (Jeremiah 2:20).*

When people are convinced of God's goodness and love toward them, they usually don't feel much resistance to His authority. But what about the authority of other people? Isn't there something in us that bucks up quickly whenever someone tries to rule over us? Everything in us tells us that we have the right to be free from the burden of authority. But what does God say about that? Do human authority systems come from God?

To answer the question, let's first look at some biblical examples where God's people needed to rebel against authority.

Read Daniel 3. How did these three young men rebel against human authority? What was the outcome?

Read Daniel 6. Describe how and why Daniel rebelled against the authority over him. What was the outcome?

David is another example of appropriate rebellion against human authority. Before he became king of Israel, David served in the house of King Saul. David was a mighty man of strength and military ability, and the people quickly realized he would be a better king than Saul. Saul, of course, became very jealous of David — even to the point of wishing to kill him. David had to run for his life, but Saul pursued him relentlessly.

Read 1 Samuel 24. Summarize what happened in this story.

At this point, Saul had been attempting to kill David for years, which makes it seem like David had every right to kill the king in self-defense. But he did not kill Saul. Why? Because David understood he still had a responsibility to respect Saul's authority as king.

Even so, notice that David *did* run away from Saul when his life was threatened. In other words, we are not expected to submit to authority when our lives are in danger. Yet David's attitude was still one of submission even while he fled for his safety.

ASSIGNMENT

In light of the Scripture reading for today, think of a situation in which you think it is appropriate to disregard human authority. Describe that situation in the space below.

DAY 4 | BIBLICAL TEACHING

Yesterday we explored biblical characters that rightly rebelled against human authority. Today, we will look at some biblical examples that speak positively about human authority, even when that authority is not godly.

Read Romans 13:1-7 and 1 Peter 2:13-15. How would you describe the main arguments in these verses?

Another biblical example of an earthly authority figure being used by God is found in Isaiah 44:28-45:3. This passage describes how God would use Cyrus, a pagan king, to help return the Israelites to Jerusalem after their captivity.

Read Isaiah 44:28–45:3. What promises did God make in these verses?

It's interesting that Cyrus was by no means a follower of God, yet the text describes him as God's servant. Cyrus was still an instrument in God's hand used to bless and benefit God's people. We need to remember that God can use a Cyrus in our lives to bring about God's blessings even though they are unaware of what's happening.

When we put together what the Bible teaches about human authority, we find several important principles:

1. We are within our right to defy authority when we are asked to violate the beliefs of our faith. This was the case in Daniel 3, where the three youths were asked to participate in the worship of other gods. (See Acts 4 for another example.)

2. We have the approval of God to run from authority that is abusive or threatening to our lives. In doing so, we must maintain an attitude of submission even while on the run.

3. Private vengeance is forbidden; we must operate within the confines of authorized officials. These earthly rulers are servants who are answerable to the one true God.

4. Christians should never assume that loyalty to Jesus gives freedom for civil disobedience, which would only reshuffle political powers. We are to live as a sign of the kingdom yet to come — a kingdom characterized by *righteousness and peace and joy in the Spirit* (see Romans 14:17). This kingdom cannot be ushered in by violence and hatred. As Christians we are to be revolutionary, not rebellious.

ASSIGNMENT

Use the following questions to help process what the Bible teaches about human authority.

What are the examples of human authority in your life?

How have you responded to human authority in the past?

Based on what you've learned, how should you approach the people in authority over you now?

DAY 5 | OUR SUBMISSION

Getting back to Jeremiah's story, it's important to remember that God clearly told His people to submit to the authority of the Babylonians. Further, God made it clear that He would use the king of Babylon to bring about His will.

Read Jeremiah 27:1-15. What did Jeremiah symbolize by wearing a yoke around his neck?

Make no mistake: living under the Babylonians' authority was anything but pleasant. God's people were still captives and slaves in a foreign land. Yet it was God's will for them to be subject to the Babylonians for a season.

We must always remember that God is sovereign. His reign is forever — far greater than those of human rulers that will come and go. So when you submit to the human authority placed over you, you are really submitting to God's supreme reign. You are submitting to God Himself.

Bondservants, obey in everything those who are your earthly masters, not by way of eye-service, as people-pleasers, but with sincerity of heart, fearing the Lord. Whatever you do, work heartily, as for the Lord and not for men. (Colossians 3:22-23)

Read Ephesians 5:21. How would you summarize this verse in your own words?

Read Philippians 2:3-11 several times. What does it mean to have the mind (the attitude) of Christ?

As believers, we have been given a realm of authority over the Devil, this world, and sin. But God will not bless our rebellion. I love the way Adrian Rogers said it: "… You cannot be over those things that God wants you to be over until you learn to be under those things that God has set over you." [1]

Could it be that you have not been able to get victory in certain areas of your life because you are rebellious in other areas?

---

1. Adrian Rogers, *The Incredible Power of Kingdom Authority: Getting an Upper Hand on the Underworld* (Nashville, TN: B&H Publishing, 2002), p. 63.

ASSIGNMENT

Spend several moments in prayer about the issue of submission to authority. Ask God to speak to your heart about any areas of rebellion in your life. Record your thoughts below.

Review your memory verse for this week — Ephesians 5:21. See if you can write it below from memory.

Lesson 5

SUMMARY

JEREMIAH'S WORLD — DEEP HEALING

The people of Judah were spiritually sick and needed healing, but the priests and false prophets of Jeremiah's day treated the wounds as if they weren't serious; they refused to offer truth to God's people. Instead, the false prophets and priests told the people what they wanted to hear.

APPLICATION

All of us carry wounds of our own. Unlike the people of Judah, we must be honest about the seriousness of our wounds and allow God to heal us all the way through. To walk in victory and power will take more than just a Christian bandage. We need the Great Physician to treat our every sickness.

LESSON 5 **MEMORY VERSES**

*For from the least to the greatest
of them, everyone is greedy for
unjust gain; and from prophet to
priest, everyone deals falsely. They
have healed the wound of My
people lightly, saying, "Peace,
peace," when there is no peace.*

(Jeremiah 6:13-14)

Lesson 5

DEEP HEALING

DAY 1 | TREAT THE WOUNDS

As we've seen, the people of Jeremiah's day did not want to hear his message of judgment. They only wanted to hear positive prophecies. In this way, they were similar to many people groups throughout history.

Read what the apostle Paul had to say about such people in 2 Timothy 4:2-4. How would you summarize these verses?

Even those entrusted with teaching God's Word — the priests and prophets — withheld the life-giving truth from the people of Judah. They simply told the people what everyone wanted to hear.

Read Jeremiah 6:13-15. Where do you see spiritual leaders keeping the truth from the people in today's world?

What motivates people to avoid the truth and simply tell others what they want to hear?

Different Bible versions translate Jeremiah 6:14a in these ways:

- *They dress the wound of My people as though it were not serious.* (NIV)
- *They have healed the wound of My people lightly.* (ESV)
- *They have healed also the hurt ... of My people slightly.* (KJV)
- *They have also healed the hurt of My people slightly.* (NKJV)

I spent 13 years as a registered nurse in the oncology field, which means I've had my share of dressing wounds. We typically think of wounds resulting from accidents such as falling, being shot, being cut. The wounds I dealt with the most were surgical wounds. The doctor would intentionally cut a person open for the purpose of removing cancer. This was all done in a sterile environment, so the surgical wound could be closed up with stitches or staples.

Without complications, the surgical wound would heal in a week or so. Sometimes, though, bacteria would enter into the area and the surgical site would become infected. One would think that the best thing to do would be to treat the visible symptoms while leaving the internal layers protected. A good nurse knows, however, that true healing can only come by opening up the wound and getting all the way to the bottom of it. Healing must take place from the bottom up. The typical process would be to open up the wound by removing whatever was holding it together (stitches or staples) and then to pack in sterile gauze all the way to the bottom. Two to three times a day, bacteria-saturated gauze would be removed and fresh packing would be put in place. This process of healing through packing and repacking can take weeks — even months. It's also painful and unattractive. But to cover the area superficially would only allow the wound to abscess and rot from the inside, causing the person to become poisoned with infection, possibly leading to death.

Just like a good doctor or nurse should not ignore the signs of infection by covering over the wound, someone who follows Christ and knows the Word can't decide not to treat the spiritual wounds in his or her own life. If you are going to have healthy relationships with your family and others, you must let the Great Physician tend to your wounds.

Such healing will be ugly for a while. It will even be painful. But don't halt the process until full healing is achieved.

ASSIGNMENT
Take a moment to consider your life, both now and in the past. What are some of the spiritual wounds you've suffered?

DAY 2 | FIRST LAYER — DENIAL OF SIN

Yesterday I shared my nursing analogy for how to heal serious wounds by treating the damage layer by layer. Over the next few days, we'll use the same idea to think about the process of treating our spiritual wounds layer by layer under God's care.

Read Jeremiah 8:4-12 to find the starting place for such treatment. What did God want His people to understand from these verses?

The very bottom level of our spiritual wounds is the denial of our own sin. Look again at verses 4-6: *You shall say to them, "Thus says the LORD: When men fall, do they not rise again? If one turns away, does he not return? Why then has this people turned away in perpetual backsliding? They hold fast to deceit; they refuse to return. I have paid attention and listened, but they have not spoken rightly; no man relents of his evil, saying, 'What have I done?' Everyone turns to his own course, like a horse plunging headlong into battle."*

In what ways are you clinging to deceit regarding your sinfulness?

What area of your life have you refused to turn over to God?

Never underestimate your ability to deceive yourself. Sometimes we are the problem and we don't even realize it. Be willing to let trustworthy people speak truth to you. Regularly expose your heart to God, asking Him to reveal to you any area of offense (see Psalm 139:23-24). Don't cling to your deceit when you find it. If the Holy Spirit brings an area of conviction to you, rejoice! He is still giving you a chance to repent. Have a regular practice of repentance.

ASSIGNMENT

Spend several minutes reading and meditating on 1 John 1:8-2:2 now. Write a summary of these verses below.

What steps should you take as you begin to recognize your own sin?

DAY 3 | SECOND LAYER — CONTINUING DESTRUCTIVE BEHAVIOR

The second layer of healing our wounds involves the continuation of destructive behavior. Sometimes we find it so hard to heal because we keep damaging ourselves over and over again.

In Jeremiah 8:4-5, the prophet asked a few rhetorical questions that boiled down to this idea: when people fall down, they automatically know they should get back up. But the people of Judah had fallen into sin and decided to stay down — they weren't even trying to fix their sinful behavior.

What are some reasons why people have such a difficult time not repeating the same mistakes over and over again?

Read Jeremiah 2:23-25. What was Jeremiah communicating about the people of Judah?

As we continue the process of healing our wounds, we must come to the point of realizing our own powerlessness to change our behavior. We can't fix ourselves. We need God to heal us of our sin before we can heal the damage of our sin.

ASSIGNMENT

What are some sinful behaviors that are causing spiritual damage in your life even now? Use the space below to make a list.

Take a look at the list of the fruit of the Spirit in Galatians 5:22-23. Which of these qualities do you most want to reveal in your relationships with friends and family?

DAY 4 | THIRD LAYER — ABUSE OF RELATIONSHIPS

As we continue to talk about healing spiritual wounds, the third layer of those wounds is the abuse of our relationships with others. If we want to experience God's healing, we must stop trying to find healing from other people.

So far we have focused on the people of Judah's sin of worshiping idols rather than God. But Jeremiah 7:3-7 reveals other sinful behaviors that were equally offensive to God.

Read Jeremiah 7:3-7. What activities did God condemn in these verses?

We need to be honest about the way we have used people as a means to satisfy our own wounded hearts. Whom have you set up to be your "savior"? This would be the person (or people) you look to for fulfillment and purpose. Guess what? They will let you down. They were never meant to be your source of happiness.

Whom have you used, abused, and manipulated to satisfy your physical cravings? These cravings may be sexual in nature, or psychological as in the form of power or greed.

How have you wrongly turned to other people to try and meet your deepest needs?

Our relationships with others must be first filtered through our relationship with Christ. When He is our love, our life, and our Lord, we will have a right mindset about others. We will see everyone as image-bearers of God, filled with potential in His capable hands.

As we grow in Christ, we will no longer need the approval of people to make us feel better about ourselves. Instead, we will be satisfied in our identity in Him.

ASSIGNMENT

Think through your current relationships and identify a person you may have wronged or abused in order to meet your own needs. Without naming names, use the space below to write out an apology to that individual.

DAY 5 | FOURTH LAYER — PAST HURTS

As we finally make it to the top level of healing our spiritual wounds, we come to our need to be healed from past hurts. This is something Jeremiah understood all too well.

Read Jeremiah 9:7-11. What was making God feel grief in these verses?

God understood what would happen to His people — what needed to happen in order for them to return to Him. Yet He wept over the reality. In the same way, God will allow you to feel the pain of consequences in your own life so that you will move out of bad circumstances.

As we experience those consequences, however, it's appropriate to mourn. Mourning can be a good thing. If we want to be healed from past hurts, we must properly grieve through them. More will be said about the grieving process in Lesson 9. For now, however, let's evaluate how we have handled past hurts.

Are your family relationships weighed down by unresolved past hurts? Consider these three areas:

1. Whom do you need to forgive for hurting you?

2. Whom have you hurt and need to seek forgiveness from?

3. What might it look like for you to properly mourn those hurts — those done to you and those done by you?

Read Jeremiah 9:7-11 again. Here we see the mystery of God's sovereignty and the sufferings of this world. God was in control of Jerusalem's fate, yet He wept over what must be done. Perhaps you have had difficulty in reconciling God's goodness with the evil of this world. Though we may never fully understand this mystery, we can rest in knowing that God is in control — and that He is just and right. At the same time, we remember that we live in a fallen world still affected by sin.

One day, with the return of Christ, this world will be set right and everything shall be restored and made perfect. In the present time, we are encouraged to remember that God sees our hurts and has compassion on us. He will not waste one ounce of our pain and suffering, but instead will work it for our good (see Romans 8:28).

ASSIGNMENT

In light of today's lesson, reflect on the complete Serenity Prayer:

God, give us grace to accept with serenity
the things that cannot be changed,
Courage to change the things
which should be changed,
and the wisdom to distinguish
the one from the other.

Living one day at a time,
Enjoying one moment at a time,
Accepting hardship as a pathway to peace,
Taking, as Jesus did,
This sinful world as it is,
Not as I would have it,
Trusting that You will make all things right,
If I surrender to Your will,
So that I may be reasonably happy in this life,
And supremely happy with You forever in the next.
Amen.[2]

---

2. Reinhold Niebuhr, "Serenity Prayer," *The Essential Reinhold Niebuhr: Selected Essays and Addresses* (New Haven, CT: Yale UniversityPress, 1983), p. 251.

MEMORY VERSE REVIEW

Lessons 1–5

LESSON 1 — *I press on toward the goal for the prize of the upward call of God in Christ Jesus. (Philippians 3:14)*

LESSON 2 — *For I know the plans I have for you, declares the LORD, plans for welfare and not for evil, to give you a future and a hope. (Jeremiah 29:11)*

LESSON 3 — *Let no corrupting talk come out of your mouths, but only such as is good for building up, as fits the occasion, that it may give grace to those who hear. (Ephesians 4:29)*

LESSON 4 — *Submitting to one another out of reverence for Christ. (Ephesians 5:21)*

LESSON 5 — *For from the least to the greatest of them, everyone is greedy for unjust gain; and from prophet to priest, everyone deals falsely. They have healed the wound of My people lightly, saying, "Peace, peace," when there is no peace. (Jeremiah 6:13-14)*

Lesson 6

SUMMARY

JEREMIAH'S WORLD: FAKE PEACE

The people of Jeremiah's day valued peace. They wanted peace. And the prophets and priests were proclaiming, "Peace! Peace!" There was just one problem: God did not intend for them to have peace. The prophets were telling the people what they wanted to hear and avoiding the real issues.

APPLICATION

Healthy families realize that peace cannot be manufactured or faked. Real peace comes from God. When we are walking in harmony with God, submitted to His will and His ways, we feel the fullness of His presence and we enjoy peace in that presence.

LESSON 6 **MEMORY VERSES**

May the LORD give strength to His people! May the LORD bless His people with peace!

(Psalm 29:11)

Fake Peace

Lesson 6

FAKE PEACE

DAY 1 | SHALOM IS DEFINED AS SEEING GOD'S FACE

We saw in Jeremiah 6:14 that false prophets were telling the people of Judah *"peace, peace" when there was no peace.* They were causing harm by encouraging God's people to ignore their spiritual wounds.

But let's stop for a moment and examine that word *peace.* In the Hebrew language of the Old Testament, the original word is *shalom,* which you may have heard before. The general meaning behind *shalom* is completion and fulfillment — entering a state of wholeness, unity, harmony, and balance. This kind of peace can only be found in God.

Here are some Old Testament passages that utilize the word *shalom* (emphasis added):

- *Let me hear what God the LORD will speak, for He will speak* **peace** *to His people, to His saints; but let them not turn back to folly. (Psalm 85:8)*

- *May the LORD give strength to His people! May the LORD bless His people with* **peace**! *(Psalm 29:11)*

- *The LORD bless you and keep you; the LORD make His face to shine upon you and be gracious to you; the LORD lift up His countenance upon you and give you peace. (Numbers 6:24-26)*

What repeated words and themes do you notice in these verses?

Look again at Numbers 6:24-26. These verses are sometimes referred to as the "priestly prayer." The phrase *the LORD make His face to shine upon you* may seem strange in today's language, but it was an important blessing in the ancient world. The idea of God's face turned toward you illustrates you being in His presence. Imagine that you walk into a room and a person is already in the room with his back turned away from you. You don't really feel like you are in his presence until he turns around and sees you.

When have you recently felt as if you were in God's presence?

This prayer celebrates God's face turned toward us. In other words, the priest prays that the people will dwell in God's presence and walk in a way that invites His full presence in their lives. Of course, God is omnipresent, meaning there is nowhere that He is not (see Psalm 139:7-10). We are never really out of His presence. He never turns His back to us. Maybe we would like Him to turn away from us when we know we are not acting as we should! But He never will.

The priestly prayer encourages us to live in such a way that we don't hinder God's presence and activity in our lives. Only God's presence brings shalom. When we choose to live in rebellion to God, does His presence leave us? Not at all. But the presence that should bring peace now brings conviction. When we are walking in harmony with God, submitted to His will and His ways, we feel the fullness of His presence and we enjoy peace in that presence.

ASSIGNMENT

Think about recent moments when you have tried to connect with God and come into His presence. Have those moments produced peace or conviction in your heart? Explain below.

DAY 2 | SHALOM IS NOT THE ABSENCE OF CONFLICT

Today in Israel, people use shalom every day as a greeting. As a matter of fact, shalom is equivalent to the English greeting, "How are you doing?" It goes something like this in Hebrew: "Is there any peace in you?"

Describe where you are right now in your walk with the Lord. Is there any peace in you?

To help gain a better understanding of *shalom,* let's make sure we're clear on what *shalom* is not. For example, shalom does not mean the absence of turmoil or conflict in our lives. It doesn't mean that nothing ever goes wrong.

Last week we saw that we can't ignore the spiritual wounds in our lives. We must seek health and recovery throughout every layer. Therefore, avoiding conflict altogether is not the way to get peace. Was there a peacekeeper in your family? These people won't allow any disagreements or conflict at all costs. While you may have peace on the surface level, the relationships really are not healthy because issues are not being resolved. Amazingly, families can live together with serious dysfunction and no one will bring it up for decades!

What are some areas of conflict or dysfunction in your family?

True peace will come only when that wound has been healed thoroughly. Are you willing to have some difficult conversations?

ASSIGNMENT

Make a list of situations that need to be dealt with in order for your family to have real peace.

What steps can you take this week to start resolving one or more of these issues?

DAY 3 | SHALOM IS NOT THE ABSENCE OF OFFENSE

Perhaps you hesitate to start some healing conversations because you know the person on the receiving end has a short fuse. Peeling off the bandage to treat the wound would only set the person off into a rage. How are you to respond to this?

Similarly, do you have abusive people in your life that always seem to suck you into their dysfunction? Your love for this person causes you to keep going back, yet you know it will cost you in many ways.

What people came to mind when you read the paragraphs above?

What emotions do you experience when you think about attempting to confront these individuals?

For both of these situations, part of finding peace is learning how to set healthy boundaries. In other words, your move toward healthiness may offend people. For the rageaholics, your probing of the wound will make them angry. They will interpret your actions as a personal attack. With those who drag you down into their messy lives, they will be offended at what may seem like your betrayal because you refuse to be part of unhealthy situations.

Given these realities, we must remember that shalom is not the absence of offense. Yes, your move to a healthy relationship may offend people. The gospel message itself brought offense. Jesus said to expect that the truth would offend some people and cause division.

Read Matthew 10:34-39 and Luke 12:51-53. How would you

summarize these Scripture passages?

Truth sometimes brings division. When we are talking about families, we don't want to end here at the point of division. We pray that the division is temporary and a step on the journey to wholeness.

Even so, you must learn how to set healthy boundaries with people. Their mess, or their anger, or their hurt feelings should not dictate your peace. A healthy boundary says: "I still love you completely, but I will not let you pull my emotional strings. I will not let you rob my joy. I will not mirror the anger or unhealthy response you are expressing to me." You have control of yourself and your emotions, not anyone else's. You can't make yourself responsible for their behavior or their reaction to truth.

While it is true that you may need to speak pointedly into a difficult and explosive situation, you should always do so in love. A good rule of thumb is to question yourself first: "What is my motive for speaking truth to this person?" If the answer is to bring about healing and growth in yourself and the person, then speak. If the answer is to help the person be better, then speak. If the answer is to put the person in his or her place, to set them straight and show them they can't get anything over on you, then don't speak!

Until your motive is love, hold your tongue.

ASSIGNMENT

Think through your current relationships. Which ones have healthy boundaries, and which ones are unhealthy? Write down both lists below.

DAY 4 | SHALOM IS NOT THE ABSENCE OF TROUBLE

Just like shalom does not mean the absence of conflict, it also does not mean the absence of trouble in your life. Jesus made that clear to us: *I have said these things to you, that in Me you may have peace. In the world you will have tribulation. But take heart; I have overcome the world (John 16:33).*

In this world we will have trouble, or tribulation. So don't wait for some magic day to come when we enjoy trouble-free lives. Even though we work to make our relationships healthy, we will still experience some form of trouble on a regular basis. Yet Jesus promised to give us peace even in this troubled world.

Read the passages below to see how we experience peace in our lives despite our circumstances.

1. Peace is available through Jesus Christ; read John 14:25-27.
2. Peace is a part of the fruit of the Spirit; read Galatians 5:22-23.
3. Peace is a position before God; read Romans 5:1.
4. Peace is able to be spread to others; read Luke 10:5-7.

What strikes you as most interesting or encouraging about the above passages? Why?

As we stated previously, shalom is a Hebrew term introduced in the

Old Testament. In the New Testament, we see a specific greeting that appears to be created just for Christians. The phrase "Grace and peace to you" occurs in almost every epistle in the New Testament. In this phrase, Paul coined a new term that linked the shalom of God to the grace of God offered in Christ Jesus.

The bottom line is this: Do you want peace? Seek Jesus. Follow Jesus. Be filled with His Spirit and He will direct you as you work toward peace and healthy relationships with others.

ASSIGNMENT

As much as you are able, spend several moments intentionally seeking peace throughout the rest of your day. Try to find time to get alone and pray, asking God to grant you an experience of shalom.

DAY 5 | THE STRENGTH OF SHALOM

People in today's world (especially men) often associate peace with weakness. This isn't true. In reality, the ability to remain at peace in the middle of all the trouble and turmoil of life is a sign of great strength.

In order to make sure you have a clear understanding of the material covered this week, provide a brief answer for each of the following questions:

How would you describe the concept of shalom in your own words?

Give three examples of what shalom is not.

Where is the only place we can find true peace?

ASSIGNMENT

What are your plans for seeking peace (shalom) during your time in prison? What steps can you take?

Review your memory verse for this week — Psalm 29:11. See if you can write it below from memory.

SUMMARY

JEREMIAH'S WORLD: TOXIC FAMILY

Everyone needs people they can trust — even prophets who share God's truth. Yet as we'll see this week, Jeremiah needed rescuing from the very people he should have been able to trust most.

APPLICATION

We must recognize the toxic people in our lives and act appropriately to ensure that they will not endanger us any longer.

LESSON 7 **MEMORY VERSES**

*When I thought, "My foot slips,"
Your steadfast love, O LORD,
held me up. When the cares
of my heart are many, Your
consolations cheer my soul.*

(Psalm 94:18-19)

TOXIC FAMILY

DAY 1 | HEALTHY BOUNDARIES FOR THE RECONCILIATION OF FAMILIES

The ultimate goal of this Bible study, coupled with additional resources from Malachi Dads, is to equip you to be a godly father who passes on a spiritual legacy to his family. God loves families. He has always intended to work in and through family structures to bring about His kingdom work (see Deuteronomy 6:4-9, Malachi 4:5-6).

As a father, you are called to take up the responsibility for your own discipleship and the discipleship of your children. Your duty toward the children under your care must be unconditional. Your love for them is unwavering. It does not fade when they fail or disappoint you. You encourage them and build them up and do everything in your power to help make them better people. You are entrusted with those children. That's why our weekly pledge reminds us of the call to godly fatherhood.

What are some of your primary goals as a father?

We have a different responsibility to our other family members — those in our family of origin (the family we grew up in), even our spouse, in-laws, and so on. Last week's lesson taught us how to work toward healthy relationships by speaking truth when needed and setting healthy boundaries with others. We mentioned dysfunctional people who tend to suck us into their messy lives. Sometimes these problems can be remedied as wounds are healed and the parties learn to communicate and relate to each other in healthy ways. That's our goal, of course: the reconciliation of families.

Other times, however, family situations can be too toxic to be remedied. We'll explore both situations in this week's material.

ASSIGNMENT

Take a moment to consider the most significant relationships within your family. Use the space below to record words or emotions that come to mind when you think about those relationships.

DAY 2 | HEALTHY BOUNDARIES FROM TOXIC FAMILY MEMBERS

We can read about a toxic situation in Jeremiah's life found in Jeremiah 11:18-23. Below is a summary of the main characters:

- Jeremiah: the prophet, delivering a harsh word from God that is not well received by the people

- Men of Anathoth: those plotting to kill Jeremiah in order to shut him up

- God: coming to Jeremiah's defense just as He promised He would. (See Jeremiah 1:17-19.)

Read Jeremiah 11:18-23 to get a sense of the whole story. What strikes you as most interesting?

At first glance, this attack on Jeremiah may not surprise you. God had already warned him that the people would hate him and his message. They would try to kill Jeremiah, but God would offer protection as long as he continued in obedience.

The dramatic twist to this story comes when you fully understand the identity of the men of Anathoth. Go back and read the first verse of this book: *The words of Jeremiah, the son of Hilkiah, one of the priests who were in Anathoth in the land of Benjamin (Jeremiah 1:1).*

Why is this verse significant to the story mentioned above?

That's right. Jeremiah's own family wanted him dead. They plotted to kill him, hoping to catch him off guard since his defenses would likely be down with his own family.

Read Jeremiah 11:18-19 again. How did Jeremiah avoid their trap?

ASSIGNMENT

As you have time to connect with God throughout the rest of your day, be intentional about praying for the different members of your family — especially those who may have harmed you in the past.

DAY 3 | HEALTHY BOUNDARIES WITHIN GOD'S PLAN

I pray that not many of you have known an experience like Jeremiah's. My work in prisons, however, tells me that some of you do know the sting of bitter betrayal by your own family members. If you feel comfortable to do so, describe your family situation below.

The home setting is supposed to be a representation of the faithfulness of God. Just as God loves us unconditionally, offering us unlimited comfort and support, doing all that is possible to bring us to fullness and completion, so our homes should reflect these same characteristics. So what's a person supposed to do when his family of origin is part of the problem that led to, or even encouraged, the actions that brought about his incarceration?

That's not an easy question to ask or answer.

For example, will you be released from jail to an abusive father or other relation? Is your "support" environment filled with drinkers, users, and pushers? Are there family members out there just waiting for you to be released so that you can join them once again in a life of crime?

Simply put, can you trust your family to act in your best interest?

Who are some friends or loved ones you do trust to help you move forward in life both now and after your release?

ASSIGNMENT

Honestly evaluate the setting to which you will return upon your release from prison. Make a list of pros and cons about that setting — a list of the good things as well as those that are harmful.

DAY 4 | HEALTHY BOUNDARIES BY SEEKING GOD'S HEALING

After yesterday's evaluation, have you become aware of certain family members you need to avoid for your own well-being? How will you respond? You may need to remove yourself and your children from these toxic environments. Think of it as a rescue mission. God had to rescue even Jeremiah out of the hands of his family.

Review Jeremiah 11:19 again. Has God revealed to you the dangers in your own family?

As if his family trying to kill him isn't bad enough, notice to what class of people Jeremiah's family belonged (see Jeremiah 1:1). Jeremiah was from the line of priests. He should have been able to trust the servants of God to speak the word of the Lord to him. Instead, they acted against God's Word, even to the point of wanting to kill their own flesh and blood.

God was faithful to alert Jeremiah (see Jeremiah 12:6). In the same way, God will alert you to the dangers within your family. But make no mistake: you are responsible to obey what He is telling you to do about it.

You may be wondering how Jeremiah responded to this attack on his life by his family members. The prophet himself offered his thoughts.

Read Jeremiah 12:1-4 and 20:7-13. How would you summarize Jeremiah's response to the betrayal of his family?

No wonder we call Jeremiah the Weeping Prophet! What a hard life he had! The ultimate point of despair is recorded in Jeremiah 20:14, which says: *Cursed be the day on which I was born! The day when my mother bore me, let it not be blessed!*

The Bible gives us many examples of God's people crying out to Him in their despair. You don't have to push down the pain. Speak it to the Lord. The prophet Jeremiah gives you permission. So do many of the Psalms. When we bring our pain to God honestly, He can bring healing and hope out of the darkest circumstances. Keep talking. Keep praying. Healing can come.

ASSIGNMENT

Spend some time reflecting on the family environment waiting for you on the outside. Pray and ask God to give you wisdom on how best to interact with your family. Write below what you sense Him leading you to do.

DAY 5 | HEALTHY BOUNDARIES IN DISCERNING GOD'S DIRECTION

In order to make sure you have a clear understanding of the material covered this week, provide a brief answer for the questions below:

Describe Jeremiah's relationship with his family.

What seemed to be the source of the problem with Jeremiah and his family and friends?

How did God prove faithful to Jeremiah throughout the events you studied?

ASSIGNMENT

Take a moment to review the answers you gave to the
questions in your assignments of the first four days of this week.
Do you notice a theme in them that may indicate the direction
God is leading you to take?

Write down any fears or concerns you have about tackling issues
with your family relationships.

James 5:16 tells us to confess our sins to one another and pray for
one another so that we may be healed. Take time now to confess
the part you have played that may have
contributed to unhealthy family dynamics.

Review your memory verses — Psalm 94:18-19. See if you can
write them below from memory.

Lesson 8

SUMMARY

JEREMIAH'S WORLD — FAMILY SHEPHERDS

Those given the responsibility to shepherd the people of Judah had failed. Instead, they withheld life-giving truth from the people, which led to the destruction of the nation.

APPLICATION

Fathers are called to shepherd their families. They are responsible and will give an account to God for the spiritual condition of their family members.

LESSON 8 **MEMORY VERSES**

*For you know how, like a father
with his children, we exhorted
each one of you and encouraged
you and charged you to walk in a
manner worthy of God, who calls
you into His own kingdom and glory.*

(1 Thessalonians 2:11-12)

Lesson 8

FAMILY SHEPHERDS

DAY 1 | GOD'S DESIGN FOR FAMILY LEADERSHIP

Does the prophet Jeremiah have anything to say about specific family dynamics? Indirectly, yes. To get the clear biblical layout of a healthy family model, read Deuteronomy 6:4-9 and Ephesians 5:22-6:4. Write any responsibilities you see that are directed to parents.

In the Jewish home, the father is seen as the "priest" of his family. A priest should be the representative of God to people, and people to God. The family priest is responsible to make sure his children have been taught the truths of God's Word. Discipleship is to be done primarily in the home, not the church. We learned in the *Malachi Dad's* study that often men had abused and abandoned their calling to their family and instead victimized the women and children they were supposed to be protecting. This, however, was never how God intended families to be.

ASSIGNMENT

Reflect again on Deuteronomy 6:4-9. Write down specific ways you can put these verses into practice as a father even during your incarceration.

DAY 2 | GOD'S DESIGN FOR STRONG MARRIAGES

Today's lesson is found in Ephesians 5:22-6:4. Let's study this Scripture to understand the roles God has established for husbands and wives.

Perhaps the call to submission by a wife to her husband seems out of date to our modern ears. Read Ephesians 5:22-33 again. What comparison is made to the husband/wife relationship?

The idea, then, is a husband loving his wife so much that he would give his life for her. That is the kind of man a wife would not have a problem submitting to, because she knows without a doubt that he has her best interest in mind. Just as Christ gave His all to make us whole and complete, a husband gives his all to present his wife holy and blameless before the Lord.

The ideal picture is one in which each member of the marriage brings everything he or she has to the table with the intent of making the other person better. The husband will delight in seeing his wife become a better person, and will make sacrifices to this end. The wife will gladly make sacrifices to see her husband achieve his goals and dreams. The husband should not feel threatened by his wife's successes, but rather should rejoice with her. Likewise, the wife will rejoice when her husband succeeds. We mutually submit to one another out of reverence for Christ (Ephesians 5:21). In the end, however, the husband will have to give an account for the spiritual health of his family. As the wife respects the role the husband has, she will encourage him to be successful as the head of that home.

Family Shepherds

God has wired the husband with a strong sense of protection and responsibility to provide. You can imagine how important this was in biblical times when a woman didn't have the freedom or opportunity to work and provide for herself and her children. She needed to be under the protection of a loving husband.

In this day and time, it is possible for a woman to make it on her own. She doesn't need the protection of man to survive. However, what do married people tend to produce? Children! The ideal situation, the biblical one, is for children to be raised in an environment of loving parents. Ask any single parent; they will tell you how difficult it is to raise children alone. Sometimes we are forced to do the best we can with our circumstances and God will certainly meet us at the point of our need. A loving two-parent home, however, is the ideal. With that stated, someone has to raise the children. Kids can raise themselves; we see it all the time. The result, however, is not good. Many of the women in my prison were forced to raise themselves with no positive parental figure in their lives.

ASSIGNMENT

Describe your reaction to the husband and wife relationship described in Ephesians 5:22-33. How do past hurts and abuses affect your attitude toward the roles within your family?

DAY 3 | GOD'S DESIGN FOR SOUND PARENTING

Let's return to the husband as the priest or the responsible head of the home. On his shoulders is placed the responsibility to provide a healthy setting for which the children are to be raised. Someone has to raise the kids. Did I say that already? Yes, someone has to raise the kids. Just as men are typically wired to be protectors and providers, women are wired to be nurturers.

My job allows me to have numerous conversations with incarcerated women every day. Overwhelmingly, the greatest source of anxiety reported to me by these women has to do with the well-being of their children. Often, they can focus on little else other than getting back home to take care of their kids. Yes, these women have many other things they should be concerned about. For example, they should be thinking about how to take advantage of programs we offer like education and job-training skills so that they can provide for themselves and their children upon release. When their children are minors, and perhaps are in the care of questionable people in precarious circumstances, these moms find it extremely difficult to focus on anything else other than the rescue of their children. In the perfect setting, a mom should have the freedom and support to be home with her children. After all, no one else can be mom like mom can! Both the husband and the wife may have to make sacrifices in order for mom to be free to be home to raise the children.

Raising children, however, is just one phase of a woman's life. Now that I am older and I have grown children, I realize how free I am to pursue other ministry responsibilities and career paths that I had to put on hold while my children were little. Why am I telling you all of this? Because we in the 21st century naturally resist a passage like Ephesians 5:22-33. But when we think of the reality of what makes a home healthy, we see the value of what God asks of husbands and wives. It's not about a husband lording over his wife or getting to be the boss that makes all the decisions. It is about a husband taking seriously his responsibility to see to his family's spiritual, physical, mental, and emotional well-being.

ASSIGNMENT

Assignment: Ephesians 6:1-4 has further guidelines for how to be a godly dad. List the traits you see.

How do children respond to this kind of good parenting?

DAY 4 | GOD'S DESIGN FOR FATHERING EXTENDED

In next week's lesson we will turn to the role of the woman. For now, let's continue our dialogue to men as we learn more about Jeremiah's world. To make the connection fully, we need to make one more side trip to 1 Timothy 3. Read this chapter now and see how a man's role in his family translates to his role over the church. Write any observations below.

Clearly, husbands and fathers who have proven themselves faithful should be church leaders. This standard, however, is expected for all Christian husbands and fathers. The apostle Paul summarizes how every believing man should conduct his activities with his family. The principle is that the man is the shepherd over his family first, and then he may be called to be a shepherd over a flock of God's people. See Paul's comparison of a father as a shepherd in 1 Thessalonians 2:11-12.

You may be saying, "That's great but that is not the spouse I have." Think about these principles:

1. Pray and support the spouse you have to become that kind woman. Forgiveness, communication, and healthy boundaries are essential for this right relationship.

2. Move toward the right kind of parenting yourself. This includes rightly relating to the mother of your children.

3. God calls upon other authorities to establish justice and protection for the fatherless. (Jeremiah 22:3).

ASSIGNMENT

Your memory verse for this week is 1 Thessalonians 2:11-12. Write down some specific characteristics of a godly father.

DAY 5 | GOD'S DESIGN IN JEREMIAH'S WORLD

Now we are ready to return to Jeremiah's world. Clearly, the men who were to be serving as shepherds over the people were not doing a very good job. Read the following and make summary statements about each one:

Jeremiah 5:5-13

Jeremiah 6:13-14

Jeremiah 10:21

Jeremiah 23:1-2

Because the fathers/shepherds have rejected their duty to guard the hearts of the people with truth, what has resulted?

Jeremiah 4:22

Jeremiah 16:10-13

Jeremiah 17:1-2

Notice the common features of the above verses. The children pay the consequences for the sins of the fathers. Because the fathers were not faithful to teach the children about true worship and obedience, the parents and the children will endure the punishment and consequences God warned them about.

What about you? Do you know firsthand what it is like to suffer because of your parents' own neglect of proper living? How about your children? What consequences have they suffered because of your neglect or rejection of God's truth?

Many of us have great regrets when we reflect on the impact our actions have had on our families. Thanks be to God, He does not throw us away or leave us in our despair! In Him, there is always hope of restoration. See the following verses that describe how God plans to correct the situation of poor shepherds. Make summary statements about each one:

Jeremiah 3:14-15

God is faithful even when we are not. No matter where we are, no matter what mess we have made of our lives, it is never too late to turn to God and give Him the broken pieces. He is a master restorer. He can make faithful shepherds. Jeremiah 23:5 says this hope is grounded in *a righteous Branch* of David. Who is this person the prophet describes? I will give you a hint. He is the one who made a way for us to be restored back to God and then gave us His Spirit so that we can be faithful shepherds. If you guess Jesus Christ, you are correct! Would you put your faith in Him today and ask Him to have His way in your life?

ASSIGNMENT

If you have had unfaithful shepherds in your life, read 1 Peter 1:18-20. Be glad in knowing that, in Christ, you can be redeemed from the empty way of life passed down to you by your earthly fathers.

Review your memory verse — 1 Thessalonians 2:11-12. See if you can write it below from memory.

SUMMARY

JEREMIAH'S WORLD — GRIEVING MOTHERS

Jeremiah uses the comparison of weeping mothers to show grief for the ones taken into captivity. The children represent the ones living in exile. The Lord tells Jeremiah that work done through the suffering would be rewarded.

APPLICATION

A mother's compassion for her children reflects God's great compassion for His people. If we cooperate with God's redeeming work while in captivity, He can turn our weeping into rejoicing!

LESSON 9 **MEMORY VERSE**

*As one whom his mother comforts,
so I will comfort you; you shall be
comforted in Jerusalem.*

(Isaiah 66:13)

Lesson 9

GRIEVING MOTHERS

DAY 1 | RACHEL AT RAMAH

Last week we looked at the role of the father in God's design for the family. This week we turn our attention to the mother. Let us begin with Jeremiah 31:15-20.

Read Jeremiah 31:15-20. What do these verses describe regarding the children of Judah?

To fully understand these verses, you must first realize what the place of Ramah and the person Rachel represent. This passage is poetic. It uses symbolism to make a bold statement. The place Ramah is the city just north of Jerusalem where the exiles were gathered before being deported to Babylon. The picture is of a mother weeping uncontrollably as she watches her child being taken away from her into captivity.

The woman Rachel was a symbol of motherhood in Judah. Jacob, the father of the 12 sons who become the leaders of the 12 tribes of Israel, was married to Rachel. By using the mother of the 12 tribes, Jeremiah relayed two images in one. First, Rachel symbolically represented a mother who has lost her children, the entire nation, to exile. Second, Rachel represented the countless weeping mothers who literally lost their children by death or through captivity by the Babylonians.

Now that you have an idea of the event this Scripture symbolizes, read the verses again.

What do you think is meant by the statement that Rachel *refuses to be comforted?*

As we continue our study throughout this week, we'll gain a better understanding of the role mothers are called to play in God's design for families.

ASSIGNMENT

When have you felt grief over something that happened to your children? Record the moment below, along with the emotions you experienced as a result.

DAY 2 | GROWTH THROUGH GRIEVING

In Lesson 5 we discussed the need to grieve our losses. Let's unpack this a bit more now. Our Western mindset does not place an importance on grieving. We tend to be uncomfortable with those dealing with loss. Further, we tend to associate mourning with weakness.

Indeed, it's true that we often feel weak and helpless when we mourn. The pain of loss cripples us and pushes us past the point of our mental and emotional stability. Seeing others in this state makes us uncomfortable and, truthfully, we want people to get over it quickly and return to a state of normalcy.

How comfortable do you feel expressing grief and loss to those you care about?

1   2   3   4   5   6   7   8   9   10
(Not comfortable)   (Very comfortable)

While this tendency to avoid grief may be status quo in America, this is not the biblical model for handling loss. The Hebrew mindset of the Old Testament understood that grief is a normal part of life and must be dealt with in a healthy manner.

Read Ecclesiastes 3:1-8. What does this passage say about loss?

We must face our grief and loss and continue to dialogue with God until we are no longer entangled by it. This doesn't mean that we let go of the memories of the person, position, or thing that we have lost; rather, we are able to move those memories to a proper place in our lives as we go on into our future.

ASSIGNMENT

Look again at Ecclesiastes 3:1-8. Do these verses cause you to feel peace or frustration?

What events from your past have caused you to hang on to grief in a way that still impacts your life now?

DAY 3 | REWARD IN OUR REPENTANCE

For Jeremiah's audience, Rachel represented all the women who had lost their children to exile or death because of the war with the Babylonians. In this way, her grief can relate to our lives today.

How does Rachel's grieving connect with the grief of those who have been impacted by incarceration?

The hardest part of my job as a prison chaplain is giving death notices. The absolute worst is telling a mother that her child is dead. That is a grief no amount of comforting can touch. For a season, the mother must refuse to be comforted because the crushing pain is too personal; she is unable to let anyone else in. Almost certainly that mother will cry out, "Oh, I wish it could have been me instead!"

Not long after I started working for the prison, I was called to give a grief notice of a different kind. An inmate, who was serving a very long sentence herself, had to be told that her 21-year-old son had just been arrested for first-degree murder. As you can imagine, all kinds of sorrow welled up and spilled over. She cried out over the mistakes that had taken her out of her son's life. She blamed herself for his fate. She wept as a mother who had just lost her son to death. She grieved over her own son's future life in prison.

When faced with such loss, we must allow ourselves to grieve. We need to take as long as is needed to weep and wail. But the day will come when we must turn and let the healing begin.

Read Jeremiah 31:15-17 again. What do you think is meant by the statement in verse 16 ... *there is a reward for your work* ...?

In the context of Jeremiah's prophecy, the people who had gone into captivity were symbolized as lost children, and the ones who stayed behind as the weeping mother. It's natural for us to grieve what we've lost. As an incarcerated father, you can identify with the pain of being separated from the ones you love.

The big question is this: what will you do to make things right?

ASSIGNMENT

The bottom line is that there is work to be done while incarcerated. And that work will be rewarded. So father, grieve your losses. Admit your role in your current situation and repent.

In fact, write down your repentance before God. Read Jeremiah 31:17-19 to help you determine what you want to say, then write your response below.

DAY 4 | GOD IN OUR GRIEF

God doesn't leave us in the dust of our sorrow. He will restore us if we let Him have His way in our lives. That's a lesson the people of Judah needed to learn in Jeremiah's day. Fortunately, God did not forget them, either: *Is Ephraim My dear son? Is he My darling child? For as often as I speak against him, I do remember him still. Therefore My heart yearns for him; I will surely have mercy on him, declares the LORD* (Jeremiah 31:20).

What strikes you as interesting or encouraging from this verse? Why?

Ephraim was the name of one of Rachel's grandchildren from way back in the book of Genesis. In this context, Ephraim refers to the people of Judah who had been taken into captivity.

You may find it surprising that God yearned for the people living as captives in Babylon — that He longed to return them to Jerusalem. After all, it was God who allowed the Babylonians to conquer His people and take them to a foreign land. God knew that such drastic actions were necessary in order for His people to turn their hearts back to Him. Yet He still grieved for their suffering. He mourned their loss in the same way a mother weeps over her lost children.

God still grieves over lost children today. In fact, as a father, the love and longing you have for your children comes from being made in God's image. God loves and longs for all His children. For that reason, we can trust Him with our pain and grieving over our children — because He has mourned and grieved over His own children.

How can you seek comfort from God when you feel grief over your current family situation?

We want to love our children properly. We want to parent them appropriately, in a way that will result in their good. As we return to Him and let Him discipline and train us during our captivity, He can restore us to proper fellowship with Him and with others.

ASSIGNMENT

Are you willing to let God create in you a love that mirrors His love for His children? How will you make yourself available to God so that He can do a transforming work in you?

How can you communicate the love of Christ to your children in order to teach them about salvation?

DAY 5 | EXPECTATIONS OF OUR RESPONSIBILITY

In order to make sure you have a clear understanding of the material covered this week, provide a brief answer for the following questions:

From what city were the exiles gathered up and then taken into captivity?

What was the name of the woman who represented the grieving mothers? Who was she historically?

How can you know that God grieves for the loss and dysfunction in your family situation?

ASSIGNMENT

List five responsibilities you feel should be expected of every father. (For example, providing financially for his children.)

1.

2.

3.

4.

5.

Now number those five responsibilities in order of importance.

1.

2.

3.

4.

5.

Review your memory verse — Isaiah 66:13. See if you can write it below from memory.

SUMMARY

JEREMIAH'S PROMISE OF A NEW COVENANT

Israel had broken their covenant with God, but God remained faithful to them. A new covenant would come which would provide greater access to God and a fuller knowledge of His presence.

APPLICATION

This new covenant was made available to us through Jesus Christ. Through our faith in Him, we are in a permanent relationship with the God of the universe. He made a way for us to know Him even while we were rebellious and blind. Through Jesus, we can experience healthy restoration with our families and others.

LESSON 10 **MEMORY VERSE**

... "I have loved you with an everlasting love; therefore I have continued My faithfulness to you."

(Jeremiah 31:3)

PROMISE OF A NEW COVENANT

DAY 1 | RESTORATION OF HOPE

God told Jeremiah his life would be tough and his ministry would be impossible. People hated him for the truth that he brought to them. Even his own family tried to kill him. He was rejected by everyone but his God. Finally, starting at Chapter 30, Jeremiah got to change his sermon from gloom and doom to hope and restoration. Brief hints of hope had been sprinkled in his previous messages, but now he was finally able to maximize on God's plan of restoration.

Read Jeremiah 30:1-11 carefully. What are your impressions of these verses?

Several statements from these verses can be connected to your present situation. For example: *... I will restore the fortunes* [return from captivity] *of My people, Israel and Judah ...* (verse 3).

What is your current state of captivity? What will be your restoration?

Here's another example: *... I will break his yoke from off your neck, and I will burst your bonds, and foreigners shall no more make a servant of him. But they shall serve the LORD their God ...* (verses 8-9).

What are the bonds currently on you that need to be broken?

There's more: *... for behold, I will save you from far away, and your offspring from the land of their captivity* (verse 10).

How do you hope God will save your children from their own versions of captivity?

Finally: *... but of you I will not make a full end ...* (verse 11).

Why is it important that your story has not yet come to an end?

ASSIGNMENT

At the end of verse 11, God says that He will discipline His people, but only in just measure. How have you experienced God's discipline in your life?

How have you been changed because of that discipline?

DAY 2 | COVENANT OF HOPE

Jeremiah 30:1-11 was written for the people of Judah who were part of God's nation. The promise of restoration was a result of them being in covenant with God. Today we will explore the idea of covenant in the Bible.

The term covenant reflects a binding relationship between people or groups of people. In our day, we tend to think of a covenant like a legal contract. This, however, does not reflect the concept of biblical covenant. With legal contracts come loopholes and self-serving clauses. With a covenant, however, the participants are dedicated to one another until death alone parts them. Sound familiar? Yes, the marriage covenant is the closest example, and is indeed a biblical covenant.

If I enter into a contract with a business partner, then we have a common interest and shared economic investment. In a marriage, however, the two people don't just have a shared interest in each other — they now are defined as family. In effect, covenant defines kinship.[3]

Before my husband and I married, I had my own family and my own life. He had his own family and his own life. When we married, we became each other's next of kin, and we established a new and separate family unit apart from the ones that we came from before. We became family to each other because of covenant.

Before marriage, we each had our own agendas. Now, as a married couple, everything I do affects my husband, and everything he does affects me. Our lives are completely interdependent, whether we like it or not! In addition, everything I owned became his, and everything he owned became mine. I bet you didn't know community property was a biblical concept!

---

3. For more information, see Frank M. Cross, *From Epic to Canon: History and Literature in Ancient Israel* (Baltimore: Johns Hopkins University Press, 1998).

**What are some ways you have experienced the power of a
covenant in your own life?**

These functions of covenant seen in a healthy marriage reflect the
concept of covenant in the Bible. While marriage is an example, it's
not the only kind of covenant. In ancient times, people understood
the seriousness of entering into a covenant with someone. Here are
some basic elements of a covenant:

1. It was active until the death of the covenant partners.
2. The belongings of each one become property of the other.
3. The enemies, battles, and struggles of one are taken on by
   the other.
4. Each partner is obligated to each other, to serve the best
   interest of the other.

When covenants were formed in ancient times, they would often
involve an animal sacrifice. The animal would be cut in two parts,
and the covenant participants would walk between the pieces of
the animal. This act symbolized the until death commitment. (For a
reference to this, see Jeremiah 34:18.)

So what does all this mean? Why is the concept of covenant so
important? Because this is the way in which God chose to reveal
Himself and express His love to mankind. He made a covenant.
Look over those elements of covenant again. Imagine the God of
the universe wanting to become family with mankind! Imagine that
God moves to obligate Himself to His covenant partners! And the
enemies of man become the enemies of God. And the possessions
of God become available to man. Wow! What a thought!

How, exactly, did God enter into a covenant with man? We will look
briefly at the main points.

Genesis 12:1-3 describes God inviting Abraham into a relationship. He makes promises to Abraham that reflect a covenant thought. In Genesis 15:8-19, we see that covenant confirmed in a traditional ceremony involving the splitting of animals. Since only God walked through the pieces, God alone is obligating Himself to bring about the terms of the covenant given in Genesis 12:1-3.

In Exodus 19-20, we see this covenant extended to the great nation that came from Abraham's line. Abraham's line becomes the people of God. As a nation, they are in covenant with God. Jeremiah's people living in Judah are of this line. They still see themselves as God's covenant partner. Jeremiah is used by God to tell His covenant partner that they have sinned and will experience judgment. But because He is faithful to His covenant, He will provide a time of restoration.

ASSIGNMENT

Read and review Jeremiah 30:1-11 once again. Note that God wasn't going to break off their yokes and save a remnant from the people of Judah just because He decided to be a nice guy. Instead, He was acting in faithfulness to His covenant. Tomorrow we will see how we can be receivers of such loyalty.

DAY 3 | JESUS' BLOOD GIVES HOPE

Does the covenant between God and Abraham's line have anything to do with us today? Stay with me, and I will show you that it does.

Remember reading in Jeremiah the scattered words of hope about one to come from the line of David? We discussed in Lesson 9 that the Righteous One from David's line is Jesus. Jeremiah's people, however, did not know this. They only knew that they failed as God's covenant partner by neglecting His commands and running after other gods. In fact, God had already used divorce language to illustrate how broken their covenant was.

Yet in Jeremiah 31, God again says they will be His people. How? Surely something must be done about the broken covenant. And here it is: *Behold, the days are coming, declares the LORD, when I will make a new covenant with the house of Israel and the house of Judah, not like the covenant that I made with their fathers on the day when I took them by the hand to bring them out of the land of Egypt, My covenant that they broke, though I was their husband, declares the LORD (Jeremiah 31:31-32).*

Note that Jeremiah spoke about the future. He spoke of a new covenant to be established at some point beyond his time. God had not thrown away His people (see verse 31), but He did plan to redefine who His people would be.

Read Jeremiah 31:31-34. What will God's people be like under this new covenant?

The fact of a new covenant meant that being part of Abraham's line would no longer label individuals as God's people. No longer would an external law determine God's people, as we see in Exodus 19-20.

See what the prophet Ezekiel had to say about the same situation in Ezekiel 36:24-28. What did Ezekiel proclaim about these changes?

Jeremiah has already stated that our hope lies in the One to come from the line of David. We can see the fulfillment of that hope in the New Testament:

- Jesus is of the line of David. See His genealogy (family tree) in Matthew 1:1-17. Jesus is both from the line of Abraham and of David.

- Jesus fulfills Jeremiah's new covenant. See Matthew 26:26-28, Mark 14:24-25, and Luke 22:20. These all connect Jesus with the new covenant. Remember the sacrifice that typically was a part of the covenant ceremony? Yes, Jesus is that sacrifice for the new covenant — a covenant between God and every person who has put their faith in Christ as Savior. So, if you are a follower of Christ, God is your faithful covenant partner! You can take full confidence in knowing every battle you have is now His, and every blessing of heaven He purposely desires for you to enjoy.

- The Holy Spirit now identifies those who are God's people (see Romans 8:9-17). No longer can the family tree or the written law determine who belongs to God. Since Christ came and brought in the new covenant in His blood, those who have faith in Jesus are given His Spirit and know to whom they belong.

Remember the letter Jeremiah wrote to the captives in exile? He gave them the following promise: *"For I know the plans I have for you," declares the LORD, "plans for welfare and not for evil, to give you a future and a hope" (Jeremiah 29:11).*

The time of restoration Jeremiah described in Chapters 30-33 is dependent on the people turning back to the Lord. God said He would be found by those who seek Him with their whole heart. We have an opportunity to know God even more intimately than what was available to Jeremiah's people. Since we have Jesus, we have access to God and may approach Him in confidence (see Hebrews 4:14-16). We have the awesome privilege of being filled with His Spirit so that we can walk in His ways (see Galatians 5:16-25).

ASSIGNMENT

The message of Jeremiah's new covenant is really a message of hope — it's a promise that points to the hope we have in Christ. This is a hope we need to share.

With that in mind, spend several minutes in prayer for the men you see every day who still need to experience the saving power (and the hope) of the gospel.

DAY 4 | HOPE GIVES HEALING

When we look at Jeremiah 33:1-16, we find a number of important promises delivered from God to His people. Take a few moments to study those promises, and then answer the following questions.

What offer does God make to His people in verse 3?

What will be the condition of the land in Jeremiah's day (verses 4-5)?

What does God promise about the future condition of the land and God's people (verses 6-9)?

What are some ways you can apply verses 10-11 to your own life?

Jesus Christ is the ultimate fulfillment of the promises in God's Word — including the promises of Jeremiah 33. Like the people of Judah, we can experience the desolate lands becoming places of praise, meaning we can see even the worst family situations be transformed by the power of Christ.

That's why it's so important that you know Jesus, and that you help your family know Him. Jesus came to seek and to save the lost (see Luke 19:10). He came to give life abundantly (see John 10:10). He came to restore us back to God by paying the price for our sins (see 2 Corinthians 5:21).

Quoting from another Old Testament prophet, Jesus said this about His mission: *"The Spirit of the Lord is upon Me, because He has anointed Me to proclaim good news to the poor. He has sent Me to proclaim liberty to the captives and recovering of sight to the blind, to set at liberty those who are oppressed, to proclaim the year of the Lord's favor"* (Luke 4:18-19).

Jesus is the Great Restorer. Put your hope in Him to restore and rebuild your family. Let His Spirit guide you in the right steps to bring this about. May your family one day praise together: ... *"Give thanks to the LORD of hosts, for the LORD is good, for His steadfast love endures forever!"* (Jeremiah 33:11).

ASSIGNMENT

Make a list of spiritual goals for your family. Write down how you hope the different members of your family will grow in the next year.

How do you hope your family will grow spiritually in the next five years?

DAY 5 | MY RESPONSE TO RESTORATION

On the last day of this study, spend some time reviewing what you've learned. Specifically, think through what you've learned that you want to pass on to your family. Use the following questions to prompt your responses.

What active steps can you take to become more involved in the lives of your family members?

What do you need to be cautious about in your present situation?

What prayer requests do you have for the following areas of your life?

    The current circumstances of your incarceration

    Communicating with your friends and family members

    Dealing with wounds or areas of damage in your family

    Seeking peace *(shalom)* in your personal life

ASSIGNMENT

Review your memory verse — Jeremiah 31:3. See if you can write it below from memory.

Memory Verse Review: Lessons 6-10

MEMORY VERSE REVIEW

Lessons 6-10

LESSON 6 — *May the LORD give strength to His people! May the LORD bless His people with peace! (Psalm 29:11)*

LESSON 7 — *When I thought, "My foot slips," Your steadfast love, O LORD, held me up. When the cares of my heart are many, Your consolations cheer my soul. (Psalm 94:18-19)*

LESSON 8 — *For you know how, like a father with his children, we exhorted each one of you and encouraged you and charged you to walk in a manner worthy of God, who calls you into His own kingdom and glory. (1 Thessalonians 2:11-12)*

LESSON 9 — *As one whom his mother comforts, so I will comfort you; you shall be comforted in Jerusalem. (Isaiah 66:13)*

LESSON 10 — *... "I have loved you with an everlasting love; therefore I have continued My faithfulness to you." (Jeremiah 31:3)*

FACILITATOR NOTES

REVIEW OF HANNAH'S GIFT AND MALACHI DADS

Hannah's Gift™ and Malachi Dads set the tone for parents to assume responsibility for being godly influences and to build a legacy of faith and hope in Christ. As a part of the Awana Lifeline™ ministry, these programs focus on becoming strong believers in Christ who will then be able to impact their own families and indeed other families. As faith in Christ changes the inmate, they in turn can be a force for change in their own families.

MALACHI DADS PLEDGE

As a Malachi Dad, I solemnly pledge to glorify God and build His kingdom by prioritizing the raising of godly children, first in my family, then in the influencing of other men to do the same in theirs. I firmly believe that my transformed life in Christ — my life of integrity, pursuit of this vision, and the pursuit of godly character — will allow me to impact my children, family, and others towards this end.

I will practice a life of daily discipline and dependence on God through prayer and the study of God's Word for the wisdom in how to "nurture my children in the admonition of the Lord." I will pursue this endeavor for a lifetime whether my children are in my home or not.

Finally, I believe that my end goal is not only for my children to walk in the Lord, but that this God-given vision would impact multiple generations to come.

So help me God.

OVERVIEW OF FAMILY RESTORATION

Building on the growth incarcerated men have experienced throughout Malachi Dads, *Family Restoration* helps fathers take positive steps toward developing healthy relationships and healthy family structures — both now and leading up to their release.

PRELIMINARIES

Whether this is a new group or one that has been together for a while, introduce yourself and have each participant do the same. Make a point to ask about and write down the names and the ages of each of their children.

You want to generate an atmosphere of prayer for one another. In establishing a system of prayer, have index cards available for each participant on which they can write their prayer needs. (Names on the cards are not necessary.) Make prayer an important and regular element of each lesson — either at the beginning, the closing, or whenever you sense the need. Many of the application questions for discussion pause for a time of prayer response. Make wise use of these cards yourself as you pray and care for the men throughout the week.

Along with a study and questions for five days of each week, the participant is also encouraged to memorize specific verses found on the summary pages. You may want to create a motivational chart with the participants' names and columns for each verse.

Allow participants to share notable steps in their journey toward becoming a godly father and highlights from their other experiences with Malachi Dads. Listen for the disappointments as well as victories, but keep the discussion brief and positive. You may want to share your own growth and struggles as a way to build trust and tell your story.

Note: You may want to have an introductory session before beginning the 10 weeks of study (making it an 11 week study).

This would include getting acquainted with each member, introducing the prayer index cards, and sharing reflections from the previous Malachi Dads studies. This would also be the time to distribute workbooks to each participant. You will want to communicate the expectations for lesson study, memorization of verses, and review of the Malachi Dads Pledge.

The alternative is to distribute the books prior to the first week so that participants have completed Lesson 1 and are ready for the discussion with the group.

FACILITATING A SMALL GROUP

Remember that each participant's situation is unique. Some may have no visits from their children; some may have a very poor relationship with the child's caregiver. Not everyone will end the program at the same place. Your responsibility is to help move each dad toward restoration with his family relationships. Resist the temptation to tell them what to do to get the results they want — don't offer advice. Instead, keep an open dialogue so men come to the right conclusions themselves. Keep praying and pointing toward the truth of Scripture as you trust in the work of the Holy Spirit.

Ideally, a small group is best with five to seven participants, with no more than 10 for one facilitator. The following notes should give you the instructions you need to have a productive small group experience.

DISCUSSION QUESTIONS

There are three major types of questions that will shape the discussion for your small groups:

Knowledge

- The response is usually found in Scripture or in the writing of the book.

- The question helps participants to observe facts, principles, and information.

- The answer will review, "What does the Bible say or what does this book say?"

Understanding

- The response looks at what it means to life and the culture in general.

- The question will begin to draw out the meaning and wisdom of this study.

- The answer will be firmly based in the Word, but guide to the question, "What does it mean?"

APPLICATION

- The response flows to specific uses of the insights that the Bible and this book have given the participant.

- The question will prompt life change and faith commitments.

- The answer will lead to specific steps of obedience to the Lord answering, "What does this mean to me?"

In your leading and guiding of this study, questions can be processed either by:

1. Answering each question as it presents itself in the text for each week.

2. Looking at the knowledge, understanding, and application questions within each section of the study.

3. Having the knowledge, understanding, and application questions guide a smooth transition from general information to understanding and wisdom to specific obedience.

The subsequent discussion notes will follow the third process. Note that you're not required to ask all available questions — choose which ones work best for your group. Discussion will flow best if you include a mix of the different types of questions and allow time for different people to respond.

BIG IDEA

Using Jeremiah's words and warnings as signposts, the participants will be introduced to the journey of building healthy family structures upon release.

DISCUSSION QUESTIONS

Knowledge

1. Contrast the false prophets' message with Jeremiah's message of judgment from God. (Answers are from Scripture.)

2. How are Jeremiah's times like our own?

Understanding

1. What did you learn about God's relationship with His people?

2. What false worship activities, false securities, false hopes, and false realities do people put their confidence in today?

3. What principles for building healthy families have you learned so far?

APPLICATION

1. What false worship, false securities, false hopes, and false realities do you want to eliminate from your life? How do you think you should go about doing that?

2. What are you (can you be) praying for now as you build healthy relationships beyond your captivity to leave a spiritual legacy for your family?

BIG IDEA

To strengthen their relationships with their children and other family members, the men will be challenged to learn and practice during their captive years.

DISCUSSION QUESTIONS

Knowledge

1. What are the parts of God's promise as described in Jeremiah 29:11-14? What does God do? What are the people to do?

2. What were some of the human plans that went astray in Jeremiah's day?

Understanding

1. In what ways does an incarceration facility compare to the captivity of Jeremiah's day?

2. What plans do you see people making for themselves when they refuse to trust God?

APPLICATION

1. In memorizing Jeremiah 29:11, what actions of verses 12-14 need the most focus and strengthening in your own life?

2. What aspects of settling in are difficult for you? What kinds of support do you need from others?

BIG IDEA

Healthy communication skills will be emphasized for the inmates to apply during and after incarceration.

DISCUSSION QUESTIONS

Knowledge

1. In your opinion, which of the Scriptures that you read and studied this week provided the strongest communication principles?
2. Which of the three communication questions asked in Day 2 are most important to you? Why?

Understanding

1. When have you seen tough times get turned into healthy relationship opportunities?
2. What do you think is the difference between sharing prayer concerns and straying into gossip?

APPLICATION

1. Which communication tip needs to be applied to your life this next week?

2. What can you do to strengthen communication with your family using the principles from this lesson's study?

LESSON 4 SETTLING IN: AUTHORITY

BIG IDEA

Participants will examine what it means to have an attitude of proper submission.

DISCUSSION QUESTIONS

Knowledge

1. Summarize the biblical teaching about the place of authority in a believer's life.

2. What are the correct responses to authority according to the Bible?

3. What contrast does the text describe between Jeremiah's response to authority and the people's responsibility to God's message?

Understanding

1. Share some current day examples of submitting to authority in today's world.

2. What are possible present day cisterns that keep people from trusting in the living water of God?

APPLICATION

1. What patterns of life that reflect the environment (Day 4) need to change in your life?

2. Have you come to a place of submitting to Christ:
   a. By believing in Him for your salvation?
   b. By trusting Him for your ability to live in your circumstances?
   c. By extending this trust to His work in your family?

LESSON 5 DEEP HEALING

BIG IDEA

Honesty will be key as the members treat their wounds for deep healing.

DISCUSSION QUESTIONS

Knowledge

1. Define each layer of the wounds that needs to be healed as described in the lesson.

2. Review the message of 1 John 1:8-2:2. What specific steps are believers called to do in the healing process, and what specific steps does God do?

Understanding

1. What is the outcome of not healing a wound completely? Do you see similar results in the lives of others; i.e., families, friends, countries?

2. Look again at Galatians 5:22-23. What would it look like for families to function according to each of these?

APPLICATION

1. Examine again the three questions about past, unresolved family hurts from Day 5. What is the Holy Spirit prompting you to ask in regard to these questions?

2. What spiritual surgeries need to happen in your life to assure that you are completely healed?

BIG IDEA

The focus of this session will be understanding how to experience and enjoy the blessing of shalom (peace).

DISCUSSION QUESTIONS

Knowledge

1. Have each person choose a verse about shalom/peace and share it with the group. (This will enable important verses to be reviewed for later discussion.)

2. What does *shalom* not mean?

Understanding

1. Where does the resource for living in shalom come from?

2. When have you experienced shalom in your own life? In your family?

APPLICATION

1. What are some areas of your life that might cause God to look away (Isaiah 59:1-2)? Remind the group of 1 John 1:8-2:2 as they continue the deep healing of God's forgiveness for their lives.

2. Look again at Numbers 6:22-26. Can you pray a similar prayer for your family? What would it say?

BIG IDEA

Recognizing the healthy boundaries from toxic people will be crucial to tackling the fears and concerns of relationship issues.

DISCUSSION QUESTIONS

Knowledge

1. What were the characteristics of the toxic people in Jeremiah's life?

2. What present-day toxic people are described in this lesson?

Understanding

1. What impact do toxic people have on a believer's life or family functioning? Using the list from the previous questions, which of these characteristics most likely show up in our lives?

2. How would you describe God's plan for families to be demonstrated today? (Check Deuteronomy 6:4-9.)

APPLICATION

1. What (or who) causes pain and regret in your life?

2. What change in communication needs to be established in your life for a healthy boundary?

LESSON 8 FAMILY SHEPHERDS

BIG IDEA

Participants will focus on God's heart for family and the roles within it.

DISCUSSION QUESTIONS

Knowledge

1. What are the roles God has established for husbands and wives?

2. What is the impact on children of good and bad parenting?

Understanding

1. Develop practical suggestions for a Deuteronomy 6 Practical Parenting Checklist. Have participants suggest how to love the Lord and have His Word on their heart in these settings:

   a. In the home (personal — *frontlets* — and public — *write them … on your gates)*
   b. Traveling *(by the way)*
   c. Going to bed *(when you lie down)*
   d. Morning routine *(when you rise)*

2. What failure in Jeremiah's day has a parallel to today?

APPLICATION

1. Prompt members of the group to pray by name for their children and their caregivers.

2. If the group is close, have them share about past hurts from Day 5 and pray for each other.

BIG IDEA

The process of grieving or weeping will allow for appreciation of God's redeeming work.

DISCUSSION QUESTIONS

Knowledge

1. What did you learn about appropriate grief from this week's lesson?
2. What appointed times or seasons does Ecclesiastes 3:1-8 cause you to think about?

Understanding

1. Trace the cycle of grief which begins with refusing to be comforted and moves to acceptance and trust in Christ. How have you experienced these stages?
   a. Denial and isolation
   b. Anger
   c. Bargaining
   d. Depression
   e. Acceptance

2. How do you respond to the idea that Jesus was/is a *man of sorrows, and acquainted with grief (Isaiah 53:3)?*

APPLICATION

1. Gospel presentation — Isaiah 53 is an excellent presentation of the gospel. Focus especially on Isaiah 53:4-6 relating to the work of Christ on the cross. If you feel able, you may want to sing a hymn such as "Amazing Grace," "When I Survey the Wondrous Cross," or another sound doctrinal evangelistic tool.

2. Romans 12:15 says: *Rejoice with those who rejoice, weep with those who weep.* Practice this verse as a group in prayer. Begin with praising God for what helps you rejoice; end by asking God's grace for the areas you need comfort.

BIG IDEA

In this final lesson, the men will respond to restoration for their relationships.

DISCUSSION QUESTIONS

Knowledge

1. What are the conditions of a covenant relationship as described in our lesson this week?

2. Trace how Jesus is qualified to be the fulfillment of the new covenant.

Understanding

1 Compare Jeremiah's message to his people with the principles of Hebrews 12:5-11.

2. Why do some today struggle with and reject the covenant relationship offered through Christ?

APPLICATION

1. Ask, "How is your covenant relationship with the Lord Jesus?" Give time for each one in your group to share about their faith in Christ.

2. Day 5 is a review of the spiritual progress and family restoration in the lives of the group participants. Use O-A-T-S to help strengthen each participant's plans for obedience.

- O — Outcome: The goals you want to see happen
- A — Activities: The events and actions which should lead to the outcomes
- T — Time: The timetable of progress with the Lord's help
- S — Systematic Checkup: The accountability which prompts growth

NOTES

NOTES

Also from Awana Lifeline ...

Hannah's Gift — The Heart of a Mother

Modeled after the life of Hannah
and her son as told in the first two
chapters of 1 Samuel in the Old
Testament, this curriculum offers
mothers the opportunity to parent
from a distance and give a legacy
of faith to their children.

Item 95241

Malachi Dads: The Heart of a Father

The Heart of a Father curriculum
provides practical, biblical advice for
life, marriage and parenting, show-
ing participants how to become Christ
followers and grow in their faith. The
Inmate Challenge DVD, sold separately,
is part of the Malachi Dads curriculum,
The Heart of a Father. Make sure you
order a copy with your books.

Item 95259

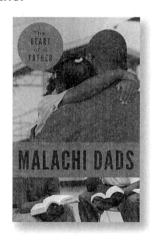

Order today!   EMAIL: awanalifeline@awana.org

Malachi Dads: The Heart of a Man, Part 1

The Heart of a Man, Part 1 is the second book in the Malachi Dads curriculum. This study focuses on how to become a man with a heart that pleases God, no matter what our past sins and failures, and no matter our physical appearance.

Item 97523

Inmate Challenge DVD

Receive a compelling challenge from some of the most broken men in our society — inmate fathers.

Filmed on location at the famed Angola Prison in Louisiana, three inmate fathers share their stories and their challenge to other inmates. This DVD is an ideal launching point for jail or prison ministry and for challenging fathers to consider the legacy they are leaving. Includes a five-week small group discussion guide.

Order along with *Malachi Dads: The Heart of a Father* curriculum.
Running time: 45 minutes.

Item 83509

author bio

Dr. Kristi Miller is an Assistant Warden at the Louisiana Correctional Institute for Women. Kristi holds a Master of Divinity with a specialization in Biblical Languages (2007), a Master of Theology (2009), and a PhD in Old Testament/Hebrew (2010), all from New Orleans Baptist Theological Seminary.